The Leadership
of the
People of God

A Study of I and II Kings

The Leadership
of the
People of God
A Study of I and II Kings

Alastair Redfern

2013

The Leadership of the People of God: A Study of I and II Kings – published by the Rev. Dr. Ashish Amos of the Indian Society for Promoting Christian Knowledge (ISPCK), Post Box 1585, 1654, Madarsa Road, Kashmere Gate, Delhi-110006.

ISBN: 978-81-8465-277-2

Laser typeset by

ISPCK, Post Box 1585, 1654, Madarsa Road, Kashmere Gate, Delhi-110006 • *Tel:* 23866323

e-mail: ashish@ispck.org.in • ella@ispck.org.in
website: www.ispck.org.in

Printed at Allianz Enterprises, Delhi.

Contents

Preface

Each year in the Diocese, I have invited clergy colleagues to read a book of the Bible together through meetings of the Chapter. It has been a great privilege to join in these study sessions.

In recent times, we have explored Romans, I Corinthians, and the Gospel of Mark

But some colleagues have requested that we also consider the Old Testament. As a result, in 2012, we have studied I and II Kings through the lens of the Leadership of the People of God. This theme enabled us to explore different models of leadership being developed, tested and judged in the biblical narrative, in a way which was able to highlight appropriate insights and challenges for our own responsibilities in exercising leadership amongst God's people today.

This small book is an attempt to share the fruits of our reflections, since each clergy chapter studied a particular part of the whole text.

I hope this sharing of our labours will be an encouragement and nourishment to each of us as we seek to be faithful in such a mighty and privileged commission – to take our part in the leadership of the People of God in very testing times.

Introduction

S cripture engages us with the living word of God – the power and presence of Our Lord and Saviour Jesus Christ. This living power means that we can 'read' and interpret the Bible in many ways – often the same passage can speak differently to different people, or even to the same person on different occasions.

As Scripture invites us to engage and be nourished by this living power, so we need to bring our own concerns and challenges to the encounter. It is in this sense that it seemed sensible to invite clergy to read I and II Kings through our need to be better formed for the task of 'The Leadership of the People of God'. This continuing task is a major theme in Kings, particularly through two models of leadership – the political and the prophetic. In the narratives, we are offered insights into the crafting of appropriate and inappropriate ways of fulfilling these challenges.

For Anglican clergy, there is a key element of our responsibility that depends upon the exercise of 'political' leadership. To oversee the organisation of a parish is partly a political task. Helping to establish the identities, aspirations

·and desired outcomes of a group of people, paid and voluntary, requires structure and systems to enable encounter, discussion and decision making. Most of us have experienced 'parish politics'! The temptation is to see these manifestations of tension between various views and possibilities in a negative light, as though the work of God will be always pure and peaceful. In fact, the sheer variety and complexity of God's creation and particularly of His human children, means that the wholeness of our life together requires careful and thoughtful 'political' organisation. The priest who presides over, or participates in, PCC meetings and other kinds of organisational activity, is inevitably involved in the exercise of 'political' leadership.

In I and II Kings, we can explore a number of models and approaches that can help us better understand our own practices and possibilities and also can highlight contrasts and comparisons with more secular models.

Similarly, there is a major theme in these narratives about the crucial role of prophetic leadership, often raised up from the spiritual and religious formation that God offers to His people. Yet this too involves temptations and pressures to accept an idealistic, but essentially marginalised, role.

In our times, there has been a strong tendency to understand public representative ministry in terms of the pastoral, the organisational, the role of nourishment through teaching and the power of witnessing through sacrificial service. All these approaches to leadership amongst God's people are important. But in the twenty-first century, our mission may depend much more directly upon our engagement in the areas of the political and the prophetic. We must avoid the temptation to allow these two emphases to dissolve into mere 'management' of the organisation and a separatist idealism about Christian belief and behaviour, so that we fail to pursue the real challenge and opportunities that the mission of the church faces.

For these reasons, I have felt this sharing of the explorations that have examined these themes from a number of angles, might help each of us to consider our own roles and responsibilities more fully as we work together in the leadership of the people of God in our Diocese.

Clearly we could have examined the books in a variety of ways. I simply chose parts of the narrative that seemed particularly pregnant with the possibilities of new light and new life for these themes.

CHAPTER - 1

Laying the Foundations

I Kings 1

The first book of Kings begins with the establishment of Solomon as King. In one sense, we can identify the process of "succession" planning, as David and some of his key advisers seek to provide proper continuity and stability for the monarchy. More significantly, we see the laying of firmer foundations of this style of political leadership for God's people. David had taken the decisive steps to consolidate the role and move from a chieftain model of leadership to one that more clearly reflected the monarchical or even imperial style of other great civilisations.

The major feature of this narrative is division amongst those in various leadership roles. As David comes to the end of his life, so the tensions inherent in any leadership structure come to the fore. Any sense of being united in a vocation to serve God's people soon dissolves into division and rivalry. Individuals and groups seek power, the people of God easily become pawns in this process.

The way in which the foundation for the continuity of leadership is laid, will be key to fulfilling faithfully the call and commission of God. In this chapter, it is clear that all leadership involves an element of 'succession'. We inherit various practices, problems and expectations. As clergy, we need to learn to handle this mixed legacy from our predecessors.

If we are too impatient to make a fresh start, as seems to be the case with Adonijah, then we may fail to establish foundations for our leadership with enough continuity and security to allow it to become the blessing that God's people should receive. The theology developed through Samuel and David made it clear that God is the King, and those raised up to lead His people do so as servants and representatives of the King. This 'political' leadership must be always rooted in a spiritual awareness and identity. This is enacted in the anointing of Kings to be leaders of the people of God.

The picture of David is poignant. The hard man, of legendary military prowess, now exercises his leadership as a weak, frail figure. It is the presence and anointing of God that empowers leadership, not the skills or strength of particular individuals. In an age concerned with competency, this is an important truth for us to remember.

David's leadership had created a problem for its future stability in a way that was to affect Solomon too. The practice of having many wives created a climate of competing interests. Most organisations, including our parishes, operate with a tension between the 'system' of leadership that everyone seems to acknowledge, and the fact that beneath this apparently calm exterior there are a number of different groups, each with their own agenda and priorities. Welcome to the world of the political!

This is especially challenging in a voluntary organisation, because instead of the centralising power of enforcement that David and Solomon were able to deploy through their military commanders, we work with interest groups who acknowledge little formal accountability and can always take their bat (and their money!) home.

Leadership in the free market economy of a voluntary organisation requires much more sophisticated skills to build and monitor commonness and mutual confidence. In the church we need to learn when to soak up dis-ease (as Jesus absorbs dis-ease and disloyalty in Holy Week, for example) and when to act decisively. We see Paul wrestling with the same issues, as he has to temper his own formation in 'law', alongside charity to tolerate space for diversity and unexpected developments.

The laying of the foundations for a new generation of leadership can be discerned by comparing the two approaches outlined in the narrative of this first chapter.

Adonijah was the eldest surviving son, and thus saw himself as the obvious candidate. He 'exalts' himself – he is ambitious. There is no report of him asking the vocational question 'Lord, can I serve you and your people?' He simply thinks that he knows the answers.

He prepares chariots, as a sign that his power will be based upon military strength – the best ordering of human resources to ensure that his human will might be obeyed. This was to be a command–control approach to leadership – hardly a reflection of the graciousness of the God who loves His people and desires a relationship of mutuality. Sometimes we can approach the challenges of leadership by organising the big battalions and marginalising any alternative.

Adonijah could be seen to exercise leadership skills straight from modern manuals, which all emphasise the vital importance of getting the right people in the right roles. He makes a strategic alliance with the two key people exercising leadership in the way that his times required. Joab, was head of the Army, a seasoned warrior and an established servant in David's system. Abiathar was the senior of the two priests. Adonijah went for the top people, military and religious leaders. He launches his new leadership at En-rogel which was a spring in the Kidron Valley, outside the city wall and he invited all the King's sons, all his potential rivals, except Solomon. Nor, interestingly for our theme, did he invite the prophet Nathan. This is a bid to establish a purely political leadership of the people of God.

It is the prophet, the one committed to keeping political leadership within the greater frame of God's call and Kingdom priorities, who initiates the alternative approach to succession. His 'word' is based upon what God has already promised through His anointed King David "Solomon shall succeed me as King".

Solomon is a very different candidate. He does not exalt himself. When the call comes, he is humble, owning his inadequacies for the task, recognising his total dependence upon God.

He is clear that the foundation of political leadership for the people of God is not power, rather it is wisdom. He will only establish the necessary power base for stable leadership after he has acknowledged his own weaknesses and been anointed with God's wisdom.

David reminds him of the foundation of such leadership. He is to summon Nathan the prophet, who will provide a critical framework. Also, he is to work with Benaiah, who comes second to Joab in leading the army, and Zadok, who was the junior of the two priests in office at that time. Echoes of other occasions where God chooses to work through the second or the youngest, rather than through the first or the eldest. Human systems must be ever challenged and reshaped in ways which make God's call, priority and oversight predominant. Benaiah, Zadok and Nathan knew about what we would call servant leadership. They knew about not being in charge.

Solomon goes to Gihon, where there is a spring in the Kidron Valley. But Solomon observes the established ritual. He is not simply seeking transference of political power; he is seeking to be placed with the sign of God's call and oversight. He arrives on the King's donkey – the King has given authorisation for him to sit in David's place, to receive David's blessing. This is an important mark of continuity and a recognised sign to the people – the journey to the place of commission is part of the process and invites public notice and acceptance. Adonijah had simply assembled a private party of key people. Solomon follows advice that places his path into leadership in the midst of public life – the people have a role in recognising and accepting him in the King's place.

Next, Solomon is anointed: consecrated for this role. The oil is a sign of God's blessing coming down – the appointment is made by God, not by a carefully assembled group of key operators in the existing system. And God is exercising His mysterious and re-forming power of choosing someone other than the obvious candidate, if judgment was made solely by human criteria. The oil is from the tent – from the place of God's particular presence and power. There is a calling, continuity and an accountability – leadership of God's people, through God's choice and blessing.

Finally, the trumpet is blown. The people are invited to acknowledge what God has done. Leadership in the parish needs to make sure that besides assembling the people God would have involved in the process and besides observing the marks of continuity and dependence, there needs to be public announcement and engagement. Leadership is for all the people of God, not just the gathered few. The blowing of the trumpet is a good test of this requirement of leadership. What is our equivalent?! The Gospel is for everyone: the outcomes of leadership need to be made known.

Finally we should note the contribution of the prophet Nathan. He interpreted the tradition, what had been done by God through David. He exercises a ministry of the word to Bathsheba, to David, to the King's advisers. He had the courage to notice what was happening through Adonijah and to challenge it as unacceptable in terms of God's will for His people. He operates as a prophet, by asking probing questions – the word of the Lord is open, exploratory, invites our response and obedience. We see the same method in his earlier challenge to David about Uriah the Hittite when he tells the parable of the lamb.

Our Lord Himself stood in this tradition of inviting people to open their eyes and see more. Then Zadok anoints Solomon: word is reinforced by sacrament. The sacrament makes public the memory of God's word. Zadok is a descendent of Aaron, whereas Abiathar was descended from the line of Eli. God's chosen way of nourishing and teaching His people is to be recognised, though it can often become obscured by the developing of human hierarchies and systems.

Solomon will go on to institutionalise the foundation for the leadership of God's people. He will build a palace to institutionalise political leadership. He will build a temple to institutionalise religious leadership and he will seek blessing for himself with prophetic wisdom. Each of these systematisations will be fraught with temptations to become ends in themselves, rather than the means of enabling the dependence of the people of God to be acknowledge and elected. But the foundations represented by Zadok, Benaiah and Nathan are important, God-given and fundamental; the priestly, the organisational and the prophetic. These three elements will be united in the person of Solomon in a way which will bring blessing to God's people, but prove too great a burden for the one called to this role. That is a picture of the opportunity and the challenge of leadership.

CHAPTER - 2

The Nature of the Commission
I Kings 3 and 5

The leadership established through Solomon was part of a process of development in the identity of the people of God. This journey had begun with a family, became a kin-group, then a series of tribes. Leadership had been exercised by chiefs, prophets, judges, and eventually a King. There remained an important dynamic between the role of the King, the political, and that of the prophet, the spiritual. Religion as overseen by the priesthood operated across both spheres.

In I Kings 3 and 5, we see Solomon establishing a stable, successful Kingdom, that for a moment seems to hold together these complex strands emerging from the traditions and heritage through which the people had been formed.

We might reflect upon the understandable desire to bring coherence and stability, alongside the sheer complexity of both the inheritance and the current ingredients of a particular situation – together with an acknowledgment that even the most spectacular signs of growth and success can atrophy and spoil.

Solomon faced tough times, with real division and challenge, yet he develops a response that is essentially inclusive of all the people, including 'foreigners' ie the basic consideration is the whole parish – all God's children need to be held in an overarching sense of direction and cohesion.

We have noted the essential continuity through the charge he received from David. Even charismatic leadership must be rooted in a given narrative. That truth underlines the importance of the Declaration of Assent for any of us taking up responsibility for the continuity of leadership amongst the people of God.

In the previous Chapter (2), there has been a 'purge'. We might feel that sometimes this is the answer to establishing strong leadership! While not advocating this kind of 'purge', which was sadly typical of the times, we can acknowledge the importance of seeking to establish teams that put the right gifts in the right places. For us, this is a vocational task, rather than one enforced by henchmen! It is vital, difficult and fraught with problems, as we seek to help identify the people God would have to share in the exercise of leadership. Too often we simply accept who and what seems to be in place. The positive interpretation of Solomon's purge for renewal of the leadership is to acknowledge the responsibility to review present arrangements, to discern new gifts and opportunities and to restyle the roles and structures accordingly. In a voluntary organisation, this is a very challenging, but always necessary, task. Solomon establishes a team to enable the exercise of leadership.

Next, Solomon marries the daughter of Pharaoh. This was a strategically smart move in terms of power relationships. But, it also illustrates the importance of being willing to work in partnership, including with those of other faiths and cultures. Too often we seek to exercise partnership with those already within our fold, or those who are sympathetic to our core aims. God's wisdom led Solomon to make a partnership arrangement with 'outsiders' too. Partnership, in contemporary terms, adds value, increases resources, enables wider opportunities.

At the same time, Solomon builds a wall around Jerusalem. Boundaries are important for successful leadership. In order to engage in imaginative and creative partnerships, people need to be secure in their own sense of space and identity. One of the big issues of our times is the dissolution of boundaries – in moral life, in ethical behaviour, in social practices, in political and economic activities. De-regulation has been seen as a positive step on the path to greater freedom. Wise leadership knows the prior importance of boundaries – discipline which gives shape and identity. Jesus was always clear in His own radical outreach that for the leavening of human kind to be effective, it needs leaven or salt that is sharp and focussed.

Most of us inherit physical boundaries – a parish, a church building. The key is how are these resources deployed, and strengthened through the boundary-giving of spiritual discipline, so that partnership and service with others can be properly effective for the gospel.

Solomon then goes to Gideon, which was a high place with pagan associations. He has been securing the home base for leadership, but he also looks outward in terms of engagement with the resource of pagan practices and places – and it is here that he meets the Lord – on the boundary, the place where worship and what we have received, meets the greater agenda of God's love for all His children. The vocation of the leader is formed in this boundary place, on the edge of what has been, what is, and what might be, in God's graciousness.

Too often, we are tempted to exercise our leadership within the walls of Jerusalem; within the home base. The point of a boundary is not just to give identity and focus, but to highlight the edge where encounter with others, with 'outsiders', takes place. That is why Jesus is always taking His gathered group 'on to the next village' and Paul keeps moving throughout Asia. Effective leadership of God's people requires a restlessness that puts the nurturing of boundaries in a healthy dynamic with the encounter on the edge. Solomon meets the Lord most directly when he ventures six miles north west at Jerusalem into a place resonant with the 'otherness' of Paganism.

Very often, it is when we venture into the 'high places' which resonate with other values and practices, that the gospel task is clarified and our witness can be properly offered.

At Gilead, Solomon had 'a dream by night'. In scripture a dream is often code for prayer – for particular concerns to be met by God's grace and guidance. We see this with Joseph around the birth of Jesus. Dream is code for prayer – deep, mysterious, not totally clear, but such inarticulate concerns met with love and direction. Solomon was on the edge, the place where the task of leadership is clarified – in a state of prayerfulness. He did not concentrate upon analysing the context, as we might! He raised his concerns to God and was blessed. In this encounter, we can see that leadership is rooted not in telling others what to do, but in being guided by God as to what leadership needs to be about.

Solomon prays for the two things that underpin the leadership of God's people. He prays out of his acknowledged smallness and unsuitability for 'an understanding mind to govern your people', for the ability to 'discern between good and evil'. He did not pray for organisational perfection or to triumph over his enemies. God's world is uneven and leadership will always involve struggle. The key is God's guidance and wisdom, not simply successful structures and systems. Leadership is not overcoming obstacles, but working with them. This is how God works with us too.

Solomon owns his inexperience and his dependency. The petition for an 'understanding mind' is better translated as 'a listening heart' – an attitude of prayer. This will keep him alive to our human context, the battle between good and evil.

God endorses this dependency and prayerfulness as the basis of accepting a commission to leadership among His people, by using one key word, 'If'. God will bless Solomon if he will work in God's ways and keep God's commandments. There is a frame given, an inheritance and a power that leadership too easily ignores as the marks of apparent 'success' seem to develop. Blessing in leadership depends upon a relationship rooted in this one word 'If'. This will be a major theme in subsequent chapters. Fundamental to leadership is not just reflection on experience – there is a prior rooting in what we would call law and doctrine – God's ways and God's commandments.

Further, in terms of a listening heart – in those Eastern societies, the tasks of leadership involved interpreting the interests of many rival groups in a way that provided common ground for identity: very analogous to the task of the parish priest!

These commissioning blessings for leadership are put to the test immediately in the story of the two prostitutes. Leadership so easily seems to be about big picture issues. In fact it is largely tested in small cases. However we want to transform our parish, the test and credibility of leadership often comes down to how we handle an argument between a couple of people. Clearly, Solomon was a leader who was accessible to ordinary people. An interesting challenge to our temptation to operate from the parish office!

These ordinary people are arguing because they need help with issues of good and evil. This wisdom is not for general guidance, it is for enacting in every human life. These prostitutes do not just need counselling, they need a listening heart and firm guidance. The world is complex and full of temptation. One woman wants to possess new life, control it, be in charge. The other is willing to sacrifice new life for the sake of somebody having a choice, out of her control, just letting go for the sake of life flourishing amidst pain and heartbreak. One wants "success" in its outward trappings. The other is willing to be "sacrificed" with inward crucifixion in order to save life.

Solomon passes the test. The one who wants justice as 'fairness' – "cut it in half – that is fair" – is exposed as evil: the one who says "no, I will give up all these just concerns, let life flourish, even if it is through sin and mess and mayhem" is blessed with a kind of resurrection. This gives us an insight into the frustrations of the Pharisees with Jesus, who gave life in the midst of sin, muddle and mess, so that blessing could be experienced despite the failure to observe the law. As clergy, we are often expected to pronounce simple 'justice' and go for a 'down the middle' solution. It is not easy to lead people towards accepting sin, suffering and sacrifice as part of the emerging of blessing and new hope.

Charter four is about establishing careful administration and organisation as the outworking of effective leadership.

Then, in chapter five, Solomon builds the Temple – the place to focus worship – a key part of the inheritance of most of us as parish priests. Even in the time of Jesus, the Temple was the prime focus and sign, and despite a history of being ransacked and rebuilt, it clearly provided an important ingredient to the leadership of God's people.

The Temple provided three key things. First, the holy space puts the worship of God at the centre of public and political life. A place which provided a reference point, a context for every human endeavour. A sign that human being must be rooted in prayer and dependency.

Second, the Temple provides the resource for being listened to by God, and for seeking guidance within the recurring dynamic of good and evil. A space within which the identity of the people and that of leadership can be focussed – from the same source.

Third, the Temple reminds the leadership and the people of God that they are all called to a commission of service and witness to the rest of God's children. The ritual and the readings and teaching all point towards the inclusive context of eternity coming with grace to embrace the whole of creation.

CHAPTER - 3

The Architecture of Leadership
I Kings 6 and 8

These two chapters show Solomon putting in place the essential structures and dynamics for the exercise of leadership – an architecture that provides the essentials of role and practice or use.

The key structure is that of the Temple. Jesus proclaims a Kingdom and says to Peter 'on this rock I will build my church.' Paul talks about a Body with a Head that provides direction and connection. Leadership of God's people is exercised within a structure, a frame, a focus – solid, secure, strong.

The word 'temple' means 'house' – a personalised dwelling. The test is to recognise who is the person whose dwelling is given focus in the particular structure. God comes to His people in the way of personal relationship. Ministry involves a personal element. One of the great challenges in leadership is to negotiate the 'role' and the 'personal' – people require the focus of an 'office' (priest) but the informality of a personal, pastoral relationship.

The temple marks an important shift – from a tent of God's presence, to a more permanent structure. This can give better support and stability, but it will run the risk of obscuring the living energy of new life that God desires to pour into His creatures. The art of leadership is to learn how to negotiate the dynamic between placedness/structure and beyondness/new patterns and possibilities.

Moreover, the simplicity of the tent is replaced by the magnificence of bold and artistic creativity. The carvings of fruit, vegetables and flowers point to the Garden of Eden – the possibility of Paradise, resources to feed mind, body, soul.

Human beings are made to come in and to go out of such a special place. Leadership needs to observe the same dynamic. The Temple exists for the world, as the world is invited to look towards the Temple. Bad leadership fails to discern the correct rhythm of this engagement and seeking/reaching out. Too often people prefer to be in the church or in the world. The primary task of a leader of God's people is to encourage and enable the essential interplay between.

The Temple provides different kinds of spaces for different kinds of encounter. The dynamic is sophisticated. First there is the porch – an entrance, a threshold, a boundary. Leadership helps people recognise and negotiate the boundary between a vision of presence as paradise and the imperfections and limitations of everyday life.

The second space is sometimes in the New Revised Version called the nave. This is the body of the house, the gathering space where people join an assembly, a congregation. Leadership enables the making of connection with others in a common space as stepping together towards the greater presence of paradise.

Finally, there is the inner sanctuary – a totally different space, wholly focussed on God's mysterious power and grace. In another echo of the Garden of Eden, cherubim guard the inner sanctuary, as they stand guard over the gates of paradise. Leadership invites the people of God to cross the boundary, be assembled with others, to acknowledge the presence and power of God in mystery and majesty.

Once again, leadership must acknowledge the one word of conditionality which frames this invitation. "If" you will walk in my statutes" (verse 12) - our invitation is to respond to what God offers – thereby modelling in the call and commissioning of our leadership the way in which God calls and commissions His people. All the verbs in verse 12 are second person singular: they are addressed to Solomon, making it clear that 'if' his leadership can engage these three spaces properly, then all people can be nourished and blessed. God's presence among His people requires the ministry of those He calls into the role of leadership.

In Chapter 8, we are given an example of how this role is put into practice. Solomon articulates and acts out the invitation and how it can be received – just as Jesus does when He incarnates the dwelling of God amongst His people through the Temple that is His living body. Christian leadership needs to hold these two sites of God's presence and power together; the holy place and the Holy Person: the common connector is the Holy Spirit.

The Temple is offered – all the people are invited to assemble, to turn towards this place of presence and power.

We have been taught to recognise this turning towards as repentance – seeking a new perspective. And for every kind of person or situation, the invitation and the blessing are the same. 'If' you turn to this place and pray, forgiveness can be offered, through the listening heart of God, and thus new life and new hope can be received. Leadership invites and models this turning from wherever we are, towards this Holy place, this Holy Person, praying our needs, so that we can be heard and forgiven and thus renewed, put into a new relationship with God and with others too. In Chapter eight, this process of turning, forgiving, new life, is offered around such everyday issues as food, conflict, sin against neighbours, defeat by an enemy, being an 'outsider', being taken 'captive' by others.

How often does our leadership concentrate upon the porch, the territory of encounter, or the nave, the assembling as congregation? How do we ensure a full turning and praying that searches through these preliminary stages into the very listening heart of God – so that as prayers rise up to Him, blessings flow down to give confidence in new life or new hope? This is the central task of leadership – to help others recognise the architecture and to engage with it for the purposes for which it was designed.

Leadership will take care to construct a recognisable porch – a place of encounter, edge, boundary. It will take care to enable people to have the confidence to cross into a greater assembly, a more intentional searching and praying, stepping closer to the heart of the mystery of God's listening heart. At one point, such is the power of the cloud of God's presence, that even the priests could not enter the inner sanctuary. Leadership involves withdrawal as well as engagement on behalf of the people. No leader can expect to stand permanently in God's presence – we are human and fallible and equally vulnerable before the perfecting presence of God.

This explains the importance of pointing the prayers of the people to God and never to ourselves. For many, especially those outside of the porch or on the edge of the assembly, there is a strong instinct to ask leadership to represent them: "say one for me". This can never be more than a modelling and such a commission must always be accepted as part of a continuing invitation to every creature to turn their heart more directly to God or to pray to Him. Leadership involves the art of representing people, but also of withdrawing to enable a more personal encounter.

A further way of ensuring a prayer focus upon God's power and grace, is the presence in the inner sanctuary of the stone tablets of Moses – the foundational framework for the 'if' of God's invitation and human response. The 'word' is present at the heart of the 'sacrament': both are vital to enable leadership and discipleship.

In Chapter eight, Solomon highlights the importance of prayer, of sacrifice and of feasting. The Liturgy which is to provide the frame for his leadership and the people's discipleship moves through key stages. Solomon begins by facing the people – the assembly. He offers his leadership to the people.

Then, as he starts to pray, he turns to face the altar. At the end of the prayer he turns to the people and blesses them. He acts as a mediator: in the language of Michael Ramsey he represents God to the people and the people to God – but only as a means of inviting more direct and personal engagement between Creator and creature. Finally, he sends the people home, to their own dwellings, to live out this new life that they have received, knowing that when they fall they can turn once more.....

Solomon uses the liturgy to model leadership that draws people in to send them out. Too often we send people from Holy Communion to an equally cosy huddle for coffee at the back of church! This can become an exit strategy from the new life just received – it is to be taken back to our homes.

Architecture is about structures to enable good living. The architecture of leadership for God's people provides a structure focussed upon the eternal glory of God, the presence of God on earth. It makes ease of access for all that cries out in human hearts. In the role of leadership, Solomon offers a word of encouragement and hope to each kind of cry - this is not some automatic blanket process, it depends upon a leadership that interprets and gives focus to each cry, so that each person can pray as themselves and be heard by God as a particular child of His Kingdom. Public worship and leadership connects the power of God with the persons who together make up the assembly. We must be wary of general systems as much as general confessions. The architecture is to invite a personal turning and receiving - the assembly is fractured or dissected so that each part can be blessed and renewed - the task as people take the gift of this new life home, is to fashion an appropriate social and economic expression of it in a collective form. Each person is blessed to be a citizen, a political agent. Leadership must understand this call and be ready to assist in its political fulfilment.

This becomes the task for Solomon.

CHAPTER - 4

The Conditional Nature of Leadership

I Kings 9

Solomon established the foundations and the architecture for the leadership of the people of God. These were focussed in the House of the Lord and the House of the King. This work was recognised and blessed by God. These arrangements are consecrated as the way to order the life of the people – a religious and a political frame. Solomon's leadership oversaw both structures, but only within the conditionality already noted: 'If' you will walk with me'. Leadership must be exercised as a spiritual journey. "'If' you turn aside from me and go after other Gods......" you will be judged and cut off'. And such are the responsibilities of this oversight that when the leadership is judged, the people are judged too, and suffer.

We can never disconnect our leadership from the life and wellbeing of other disciples. Leadership is never a 'personal' role for which we need skills that develop our own competencies, with outcomes measured by organisational performance. Leadership involves accepting responsibility for the cries in the hearts of the people of God.

But, as we see in the case of Solomon, the temptation is to gain confidence from the walk with God, and then operate the structures according to the most immediate factors, such as the need for harmony, security and stability and thus fail to interpret the deeper currents of temptation and disease in the hearts of the people, both within the gathered group, and amongst those in other cultures and faiths. The incident with King Hiram of Tyre being disappointed with the cities he had received from Solomon illustrates the diversity of values and opportunities which leadership constantly encounters. These challenges are not simply to be managed through adjustments to arrangements for exchange and negotiation – they must primarily be explored as part of the walk with God that acts to test, refine and re-form leadership and its possible outcomes. God offers other resources beyond the worldly models that Egypt and Tyre might suggest. The temptation will be to operate according to the fashions and values of the times. Whereas the love and grace of God desires to be forgiving and ever more inclusive. Leadership operates in this tension.

Although empowered and blessed by God, and working in this way, Solomon begins to consolidate his leadership position by means of well recognised contemporary stratagems. He conscripts forced labour, he embarks on an ambitious building programme, he isolates foreigners and develops hierarchies of power to ensure efficient organisation. This is a programme of growth and the expansion of power. It is characteristic of many rulers seeking that elusive cocktail of stability and success.

But, we should notice the beginning of a subtle shift, away from the inclusive grace that Solomon proclaimed at the dedication of the Temple, whereby even foreigners could pray and receive forgiveness and new life. Now outsiders are oppressed and excluded. Their spiritual journey became one of suffering, rather than the invitation to inclusion. Solomon had been given a Kingdom vision in the Temple of a God who desires to manifest love that can be poured into all His children, not just towards those who conform to a particular way of ordering the household of faith.

In his pursuit of growth and welfare, Solomon mirrors the operations of every political leader. These are the twin aims of many churches too. But the pursuit of growth and welfare raises important issues about identity and inclusion. It is not surprising that in twenty first century Europe, there is especial concern about slavery (human trafficking) and immigrants (outsiders). Political leadership pays lip service to the importance of social cohesion, but most organisations work through the dynamic of who is 'in' and who is 'out'. That is how we handle difference – by structures and values, which include some, but necessarily seem to exclude others. Democracy works through association with a particular political party.

This very human model of political leadership becomes the template for religious groups. Growth and welfare – of individuals and of the institution- are pursued through a structure of beliefs and behaviour which operate by inclusion and exclusion. This seems to 'work' because it is the quickest way to meet the deep cry from every human heart for identity and security. Solomon's strategy seems persuasive and was certainly effective in the short term, but it was not a proper political outworking of the revelation he received in the Temple, when he raised his hands and offered blessing and teaching to all who would 'turn' towards that Holy Place as the dwelling of God's Holiness.

For our own leadership, the temptation of handling the 'politics of the parish' will involve the similarly attractive appeal of growth and welfare delivered by inclusion and exclusion. The focus and measure becomes the gathered group – the church. The wider communities of the whole parish, although legally included under our leadership responsibilities, soon became secondary and then unrecognised – the concern of other 'leaders' and structures.

Solomon was invited by the 'if' to walk with the Lord who longs to include 'others' and their 'otherness'. Not by immediate conformity to a certain orthodoxy of belief and behaviour developed by a particular religious group - but by simply lifting up their hearts to the Lord, whose listening heart hears our prayers and responds with forgiveness and new life – into the places and people we are currently. This was an amazing feature of the ministry of Jesus – the forgiveness and blessing and healing so generously given in passing encounters, where He heard the cry of the heart and responded – but did not insist upon any kind of joining or conformity with His gathered disciples. There were 'degrees' of discipleship that disappeared into people and situations beyond any available radar or tracking system.

Leadership as exemplified by Solomon involves ordering the Household of God's children, from the world to the porch to the nave to the inner sanctuary. Grace can be met at any point on this spectrum though the invitation to 'come and see' is always to be offered. Each invitation and encounter is part of a spiritual journey: the spirit seeking solace and direction: the grace of God offering forgiveness and new life.

Yet the prevailing models of political organisation will have a huge influence upon all who inhabit a particular culture. These models will provide 'false gods' in terms of ministry to the cries of the human heart, and false architecture for leadership. What is so often lacking is that basic spiritual conditionality 'if'..... and 'then'. If we remain faithful to the spiritual journey, which is part of our commissioning into the leadership of God's people, then there can be blessing for His people. If we only follow a superficial walk with the Lord and too easily accept and trust in models of our times that seem proven to deliver growth and welfare, then the people will suffer and be disappointed.

This is where the voice of prophecy becomes so important – reclaiming the focus on seeking forgiveness (because we are ever aware of our weakness and failings, as Solomon at the moment of his commissioning) and on receiving new life – which will include further inclusivity and a deeper binding of differences in the grace and goodness of God.

Thus a key test of political leadership lies in the way we handle otherness. Those who somehow have different views and values. We have the example of Jesus with the Syrophoenician or the publican or the woman taken in adultery. Solomon had been inspired to stand in this place of invitation and inclusivity – but he did not stay close enough to the Lord on his spiritual journey to ensure leadership that reflected this Gospel - of which public worship was the witness and the exemplar. Once we succumb too easily to the shaping of hierarchy, inclusion and exclusion, slavery and the hunger for trade/exchange to accumulate wealth, then the Household becomes structured along the lines of human empire, rather than the Temple of God's gracious holiness.

Leadership of God's people will accept gradations rather than differences that exclude. It will offer an architecture of invitation and inclusion – from a distance by simply turning in prayer, or by crossing the threshold of the porch and joining the assembly in its more disciplined spiritual intentionality. This kind of leadership is charged to develop a new kind of community – connected in prayerfulness, owning limitation, desiring new life, dependency upon God before any structures of organisation. Leadership involves inviting others into a spiritual journey. The necessary structures to hold and give direction will have an essential openness, porosity, an ability to enhance and to be re-framed. There will be a basic commitment to being self-critical, confessing failings and seeking God's guidance and reshaping: being open to the prophetic.

In this chapter, we see the inspired leadership of Solomon beginning to atrophy uncritically into more traditional strategies for growth and welfare: to the benefit of some and through the oppression and exclusion of others. Despite the Temple, leadership was walking more lightly with the Lord.

CHAPTER - 5

The Structure of Wisdom

I Kings 10

W ith the visit of the Queen of Sheba, we see a powerful demonstration of Solomon as a wise leader – a successful political leader. The succession from David has been established (the commission from God has been accepted), the architecture of oversight has been constructed and the issues surrounding the spiritual work with the Lord to enable such leadership to bring blessing have been identified.

At this point, when security and stability, growth and welfare, seem to be in place, the Queen of Sheba arrives as a kind of external auditor. She is a visitor from the East, the traditional site of wisdom and imperial success. She comes as Queen, a leader of her people and a person well-qualified to conduct an audit of Solomon's achievements. He had begun his leadership by asking God for wisdom and this is the basis of his widespread fame ("fame due to the name of the Lord" as the text makes clear). This is how his leadership is manifested and experienced: a fulfilment of God's commission and promise. Traditionally, wisdom was to be found in the East, as we find with the story of the Magi. Little Israel would be seen as a cultural and intellectual backwater compared to the great civilisations of Syria, Persia and Egypt. The Queen of Sheba represents this wisdom and political sophistication, bringing magnificent gifts as a sign of how much power and wealth was thereby generated.

She came with a great retinue – her own household. Solomon's leadership, rooted in Godly wisdom, creates a reputation, a witness to something that others desire. Yet the Queen begins with confidence in her own traditions and standing. She begins with spirit and asked Solomon questions. His ability to explain is impressive. But what clinches the witness that he makes is the ordering of his household and the offerings that he offers. His inner 'wisdom' was clearly and demonstrably translated into appropriate organisation and impressive worship. True wisdom is made manifest in these two basic ways of shaping and valuing human life – the political and the religious. In Solomon, there is an inspiring coherence – and the result is that "there was no more spirit in her". The Queen had to own the limitations and failures of the wisdom she had previously encountered. Now she observed leadership that combined political and theological insight and a balanced outworking in terms of organisation and worship.

Wisdom is not just the Holy Grail sought by modern science – of answers to the big questions about life and its meaning. Wisdom is a quality of spiritual engagement and reflection that makes itself manifest in the political arrangements of the King's Household and in the public worship he has established in the House of the Lord. This offers an interesting test for our own leadership – wisdom emerging from our spiritual journey, which inspires insightful interpretation of the questions asked by thoughtful humanity and made manifest in good organisation and moving worship. Quite a challenge to a tendency in some of us to face challenges by implying that our proper role is to offer 'spiritual' wisdom and to claim that we were not asked to oversee the efficient management of an organisation! In Solomon, God's wisdom provides the resources for a coherent approach to political and religious leadership, in a way that offers an important witness to those immersed in more worldly systems of seeking success.

The fact that 'there was no more spirit' in the Queen of Sheba indicates a moment of conversion. She owns a transfer of allegiance and confidence to a new kind of wisdom, issuing in beauty, order and the conjoining grace of representative worship. But she needed to experience this new life and not just hear about it from afar. 'I did not believe until I saw it with my own eyes'. This highlights an important aspect of how we exercise leadership for mission. Besides the need for more intelligent apologetic in a world with large areas of religious illiteracy, there is a more important task of engaging with all of the questions people want to raise, within the context of a Household which is self-evidently blessed in its organisation and in its worship. How often do people dismiss the gospel because the witness of our church is one of disorder and worship characterised by division and difference about the offering, who is involved, how it works, who it is for. There is an important message about mission through right order – of the church as God's people, and of our worship based upon offering. Some churches share the peace in the middle of the service, but too often this seems like an idiosyncratic moment of acted out inclusivity rather than a normative sign of Christian action in the world.

The congruence of management and worship is equally challenging. Too often we designate 'management' as a worldly agenda and seek security in the narrower household of God, enacted through participative praise and worship. Solomon offers a more challenging model of leadership. The management of the household is of equal importance with the offering of worship in manifesting the wisdom of God being poured into the fullness of human life. Worship is always, as we have seen, in a robust dynamic with the management of human lives. Religion and politics inform each other through the common and fundamental agenda of needing to cry out for forgiveness and new life: the gift of the latter is only to inform the former. The spirit is always being made flesh. This is the wisdom encountered by the Queen of Sheba, and the heart of the task of the leadership of God's people.

Her witness continues, "happy" are your wives and servants and other members of this rightly ordered household. She observes not just systems that are working well, but systems that are freeing people to be who they are called to be. Wisdom issues in vocational fulfilment – as the bedrock of public life that issues in 'justice and righteousness' – a proper mutuality. People flourish because of the quality of the organisation that the leadership establishes.

Each priest is a vocation's adviser. We call out discipleship. The test is – discipleship called out into what kind of 'household'? The inclusive public spirituality of articulating the cry in each human heart, which Solomon was inspired to proclaim at the dedication of the Temple, offers a forgiveness and new life that can inspire people to inhabit a common household in "justice and righteousness". The outsider from Sheba has been allowed to become an honorary member, so that she can go back to her 'own' people as a witness herself. The outsider is made an apostle for the sake of God's greater kingdom.

As a leader, Solomon provided not just 'answers' but also a framework within which all kinds of people could flourish. Can outsiders look at our organisation and the worship which sustains it and say 'there is an enactment of justice and righteousness'? There is a stern test for the leadership of the people of God.

Resulting from her encounter the Queen gives to Solomon a large amount of money. Outsiders will contribute to the Household if it is seen to be worthwhile. This needs to be a more intentional part, not just of our witness, but also of our generation of income streams!

Finally, the Queen of Sheba departs to her own land, with her own household. Many who encountered Jesus had a profound experience of conversion, but were sent back to their own context and community to bear a witness to their new life in God's grace and goodness. Our leadership should be measured not simply in terms of those who 'join' but equally in terms of those we 'touch' but allow to go away to their original context and community. A statistical challenge! But a very important perspective in understanding the roundedness of leadership that God raises up for the sake of all His people. Insiders and outsiders can still be joined in a common spirituality of recognising and appreciating justice and righteousness.

Then in the remainder of the chapter, we see that other kings came to Solomon too. He establishes a school of leadership! He taught and traded with other rulers. He became a model that others wanted to emulate. But there is a vital distinction. The Queen of Sheba experienced both his household organisation and his worship. Others came for the former only – the quick fix for effective political leadership that the world so desperately craves. We have seen this phenomenon in recent decades as leadership theory has ransacked the language and symbols of spirituality (the 'mission statement' syndrome) but with no appreciation of its rootedness in the worship of 'offering'. Solomon colludes with this quick fix, shallow approach, by concentrating upon the trappings and immediate structures of effective organisation.

Good leadership is not sustainable in a fallen world if the bedrock of the spiritual journey is neglected. Even more seriously, at this moment of worldly triumph as a great leader, Solomon begins to show signs of succumbing to a more worldly agenda. He builds a throne for himself. It had 'six steps'. Elevation is the temptation and the downfall of every successful leader. Others collude by putting us on a pedestal. We reinforce this understandable instinct in order to increase the dynamic of success. In fact, Solomon has shifted the basis of his leadership from standing before God and the people, as mediator and as model of humble dependence, to sitting in splendour in an elevated role where he is now focus and judge. The determinative presence of the inner sanctuary as sign of the mystery and greatness of God has disappeared. Instead Solomon sits alone, the sole focus of wisdom and power. The organisation of the Household now focuses on him. The place of public worship is mere ritual, a background of little serious import.

The very success of his leadership both political and religious, has led to his downfall. He has become a leader – rather than a servant of God and of the people, raised up to enable a deeper connectivity between God and His people – in all their various grades of conscious engagement or unconscious separation. Grace can permeate every person and every place, if the task of the leader is to encourage the ownership and articulation of the cry of the human heart – and help direct this spiritual life towards the listening heart of God. A good leader needs to be ever seeking to be invisible. Marks of success can propel us into a style of leadership which brings suffering and chaos, rather than blessing and wholeness.

The focus becomes more clearly centred on Solomon himself. The next chapter begins 'Solomon loved many foreign wives;" God had called him, ordained him, graced him, and yet.....such was his success that there was no one to challenge him. A politician without a prophet.

CHAPTER - 6

∂he ∂emptations of ∂eadership
I Kings 2

H aving achieved all the hallmarks of success as a leader, Solomon is now shown as beginning to own the shallowness of his spiritual journey and the consequences for his effectiveness amongst God's people. His political leadership has not been challenged or refined by any kind of prophetic element and thus he has succumbed to the temptation to measure himself only against his own standards and those of his peers and contemporaries. The deeper and richer agenda of God's concern for all His children has become steadily obscured by the apparent success of Solomon's organisation and strategy. On the surface, there is peace and prosperity, stability and security. In reality, as we have seen, the situation has become far more precarious and in this final narrative, we see these problems beginning to surface.

However, we should note that God remains faithful to His promise to Solomon, even though he has broken his side of the covenant and withdrawn from the closer walk with the Lord that he had been privileged to experience. There is something about the miracle of God's graciousness in this fact, as well as a reminder that the worship of "offering" should be foundational to every step of the spiritual journey through which effective leadership is formed, sustained and constantly re-formed. Solomon has tried to be the Good Shepherd who organises the flock and cares for them – the political role – but, he has failed to pursue the prophetic agenda that the House of the Lord was consecrated to honour - that is the invitation to outsiders to also turn and be blessed with forgiveness and new life.

The presenting issue is that Solomon "loved many foreign women". Echoes of the Garden of Eden, where self-expression through the lust for knowing and controlling obscures the innocence of the creature before the Creator. Self gets in the way and the natural communication is fractured. This process had begun to happen in Solomon's spiritual life. It is now acted out more clearly and publicly. The desire of the self to preserve and develop itself on its own terms is, according to Augustine, the basis of human sinfulness – putting self at the centre and God on the margins.

So for Solomon, his heart turned away from the one true God to many other gods, in order that he could advance his relationship with his wives more fruitfully. Each wife probably represented an important alliance with an interest group or kingdom and thus there would have been a political as well as a purely sexual agenda. His strategy of generosity and tolerance towards those of different views and values – in the name of love – raises important issues for our world of toleration towards difference and diversity, also in the name of love.

The scenario could almost be described as proto postmodernism – everyone had a right to their own god and the task of the state is to honour diversity and create conditions in which each can flourish on their own terms. Solomon certainly supported an Established Religion, based on the public worship of the House of the Lord, but also gave positive affirmation to other faiths and practices too. In the Gospels, both Jesus and Paul bear witness to a love that reaches out to the 'other' to find common ground in the love of God. But this was different from entering into idolatry on the terms of other gods.

The question raised by Solomon is – how does leadership witness to a love of the stranger which seeks to find common ground in God's goodness and grace, and yet not to do this in a way which marginalises and obscures the One who made the world and everything in it. Amongst the gods honoured by Solomon was Molech, to whom children were sacrificed. We entered a similar situation in the twentieth century. Almost immediately after the World Missionary Conference in 1910, which was a great expression of confidence in Christianity being the normative gospel for everyone, came the First World War. Notions of empire were shattered, and out of the ruins there was a progressive redevelopment towards what came to be called multi-culturalism. A tolerant, generous recognition of difference as enriching, in a way that gave priority to avoiding conflict in order to maintain a pragmatic peace. The disaster of the new religions of fascism, socialism or communism, reinforced this movement after 1945. Toleration was the pragmatic way to peacefulness. Solomon could be seen as an early example of this kind of political leadership.

This whole movement has been reinforced by the emphasis upon individual human rights. Toleration increasingly collapses under the stress of giving uncritical freedom to such a diversity of views and values. The agenda is set by who people think they are, and being positive about different positions – a huge shift from calling upon everyone to begin their search for identity and connection by turning to seek forgiveness, being changed in order to receive a new and therefore different life.

Solomon increasingly concentrated upon the present, and the pragmatism that kept people happy. This was a genuine form of love. But it was love for humanity in our broken incompleteness, powerfully expressed by the multitude of gods and practices. Solomon had been introduced to a different kind of love – sacrificial rather than selfish, humble and aware of its smallness rather than confident and combatitive to preserve what it seemed to have achieved.

Jesus began His ministry with the word 'Repent' – turn round and cry out to God. Without this foundation to leadership, there will be an uncritical toleration that abandons any notion of common standards for morality or wisdom. Peaceful practice becomes the primary priority.

Ironically, the less of a common framework, the more explosive the world becomes. Surely that is the story of the early twenty-first century, as it was the narrative for Solomon's last years. The freedom created by uncritical toleration becomes the freedom to be disruptive and destructive. This highlights the danger of political leadership adopting a predominantly pastoral role – a soft kind of all-embracing love – a 'feeling' with little content in terms of standards or boundaries. The porch becomes redundant in such an ecology.

We may no longer have child sacrifice to the gods, but we have a frighteningly high level of child abuse and sexual exploitation. The gods simply change their names – the theologies which allow gratification of selfish human instincts simply get re-written in the contemporary language. There may be laws to try and control such behaviour, but there is little in the way of a climate of public moral values that makes it difficult for people to express themselves in such sexually oppressive ways.

God tries to witness to His faithfulness and the inclusivity of His love, but exercises judgment on selfishness and disobedience. The 'if' has real content and real consequences. God offers love in the form of a covenant. Human creatures must turn towards Him and cry out from their hearts, to encounter His faithfulness. God raises up leaders to provide the structures and points of focus to encourage and enable this encounter – the architecture of salvation.

Because Solomon reduces his leadership to an easy going tolerance of human views and values, unchallenged by owning the need for forgiveness and a new life –the Lord raises up adversaries. Toleration breeds intolerance. Haddad and Rezon are both schooled in Egypt – the alternative centre of successful political and religious leadership. The beginning of prophetic challenge is sometimes raised up through outsiders, pagans, those of very different approaches. As with Cyrus in the Book of Isaiah, God's use of 'outsiders' to challenge His people is not an uncritical endorsement of their pagan faith. Rather it is inviting the leadership of His people to recognise their failings and to consider alternatives – not least the tradition in which they were formed and commissioned. Both Moses and Jesus were symbolically formed in Egypt. The outside perspective can bring important insights to better illuminate the will and ways of God in a particular situation.

Then God raises up a prophet, Ahijah the Shilonite, who finds Jeroboam on the road – at a moment of transition, the place where new insights can be received more easily. Ahijah offers an interpretation and a critique of the present leadership. It is not comprehensively worked out or argued. Rather he offers a prophetic action, the tearing of a garment into twelve pieces. The action is a sacramental moment wherein Jeroboam is called and commissioned for an alternative leadership of 10 of the tribes – because Solomon "has forsaken" the Lord.

Prophecy often works through fraction. That is the secret of the power of the Eucharist. Human self-centredness and schemes are broken up in order to be re-membered through God's forgiveness and new life. The Eucharist is a weekly rending of ourselves, an act of prophetic critique that, if we will receive it, becomes a call and a commission to renewed leadership and witness.

God's wholeness comes through a leadership that allows the fraction induced by turning towards the holy of holies with the cry of the heart.

Ahijah re-emphasises that despite Solomon's perversion of his leadership role, God will be faithful and will honour His promise to David. The conditionality of the 'if' is grounded in grace and generosity. There will be continuity as well as a necessary discontinuity in the provision of leadership. It is a helpful challenge sometimes for each of us to consider whether our current call in leadership resides in continuity or discontinuity. Both are important and either can be valid.

Solomon, through his success and through his failures in leadership, illustrates three key lessons that we could consider further. First, the choices leadership needs to make must be rooted in the heart – in walking in the way of God - in a spiritual journey. This is a very different context from one determined by rational calculations and evidence, which together suggest an easy toleration as the key to maintaining a pragmatic peace. Worship takes us into a very different place, where easy tolerance and self-righteous intolerance are both challenged by an invitation to turn and cry out for something more. The discipline of worship is foundational to root leadership in the heart – not just the head.

Second, the choices of leadership are rooted in tradition. We recognise that we are to be shaped through a God who acts with consistency, with a consistent message about the gift of common ground in universal goodness and grace. There are many examples to inspire and encourage. Hence the importance of theological study and reflection, alongside worship. The Bible remains the basic leadership manual.

Third, the choices of leadership must be rooted in the conditionality expressed so sharply by the word 'if'. This is the place of challenge, critique, consistency. 'If' the worship and the tradition are faithfully pursued, the blessing emerges. 'If' is the demand for regular reviews, against the Temple and against the tradition. The prophetic element of leadership emerges from giving priority to the 'if'.

CHAPTER - 7

The Challenge of Prophecy
I Kings 12 and 13

Solomon had established a successful scheme of political and religious leadership for the people of God. He had been blessed with wisdom and invited to pursue the spiritual journey through which he could consistently consider the 'if', the covenant relationship of love and mutual offering that God desired to provide for him. But he was not able to maintain this discipline of reflective, prayerful leadership. His systems of organisation provided the outward trappings of effective organisation for the people of God, but his heart became increasingly self-centred –not least because there was no-one to challenge him. This is the danger of over-successful leadership.

On the death of Solomon, Jeroboam took over the leadership of the ten tribes, after Rehoboam, the son and heir, had made a disastrous political miscalculation about the style of leadership he was to adopt. Instead of following the advice of the elders and offering a relationship of mutuality and service, he decided to accept the strategy of his younger peers who proposed a show of personal strength. The people rebelled and Jeroboam had to retreat to Jerusalem, his Kingdom broken. Clearly, beneath the surface of apparent success, many people in Solomon's time had been disaffected by his policies and practices. It is often when there is change in leadership arrangements that such tensions are made manifest.

Rehoboam is faced with the task of giving the people a renewed identity and confidence. Besides political organisation, he realised the importance of making provision for religious needs so that public worship could continue to provide harmony. He decided to create a local focus, instead of the Temple at Jerusalem. The holy of holies was established in the form of golden calves – modelled on the fertility gods of Egypt and other civilisations. This was a religion to enable people to seek blessing – the politicians immediate concern – it no longer predicated a preparatory stage of turning to God, crying out from the heart, owning failings, and receiving forgiveness as the foundation for a renewed life. The new religion was much more directly attuned to a direct negotiation with the god for fertility and blessing. There was no space for the critical challenge of the prophetic, based upon the character and revelation of God. Religion was to be more directly an agent of helping people to thrive in a more narrowly political system of organisation and negotiation.

The key aim of this worship of the Golden Calves was to encourage 'growth' – harmony with the rhythms of nature to ensure fruitfulness. These gods had a very 'secular' focus, to bless human flourishing. There was a calf in the north at Dan and one in the south at Bethel – the latter location having useful associations with Abraham and Jacob.

Of course the 39 Articles highlight the value of the local congregation, but only as part of something much greater and more mysterious. Prophecy can never be localised, as Jesus told his fellow citizens in Nazareth.

Further, Jeroboam establishes a new priesthood not connected to the tradition, but a more functional public ministry designed to oversee the new religion.

As all the arrangements are put in place, to design a political and religious settlement carefully attuned to the needs of the people, Jeroboam prescribed a festival, rather as Solomon has designed and built the Temple and then summoned the people to a special service of dedication. As the political and religious leader, Jeroboam presided and stands at the altar to offer incense – the sign of the prayers of the people and the blessing of the God being mingled. Suddenly, and quite unexpectedly, in this neat and carefully designed ecology, a prophet who had come out of Judah, challenges this whole enterprise and pronounces God's judgment upon it. Politics and religion have been found wanting.

The prophet comes out of Judah, Jerusalem, the true focus of God's revelation and presence. This is the touchstone for true religion, which will provide a critique of merely political leadership and organisation. The prophet is one person, standing over against Jeroboam and the whole assembly, who were conforming to the new arrangements for encouraging self-sufficiency. Prophecy represents not just the roots of God's truth, but the remnant, the salt and leaven that God keeps alive in order to offer change and renewal to His people when they have succumbed to the temptation to deviate from the spiritual journey and make their own arrangements.

Prophecy emerges from a certain set-apartness – a sense of distance from present arrangements in order to offer a larger perspective. The problem for the parish priest in our call to offer both political and prophetic leadership lies in this tension between the need to be close to people and the need to step away and ask God to help us see differently, more in the perspective of God's greater and more inclusive agenda.

The prophet pronounces that judgment will be made on these new arrangements; both the personnel and the practices will be brought down. Rehoboam, enacting his complete power to re-fashion politics and religion, stretches out his hand to point to the interloper to be seized, and is in fact paralysed. All these new arrangements for human flourishing are in fact bankrupt, without real life. Instead the power of God burns up the altar as a sign of the mystery that new life arises from the destruction of human creations that lead to the assumption of an identity and confidence of their own, without the humility and dependence that maintains engagement with the spiritual journey.

The King immediately asks for healing –and the prophet is gracious, he is an agent of goodness. The prophet prays to the Lord and the King's movement is restored. Jeroboam as the Lord's anointed, has been taken through the spiritual process that enables new life – he needs to remember and recognise not only his own call and anointing, but the roots of this wisdom and the way that it works amongst fallen humankind. As a leader, he too had succumbed to the temptation which had ensnared Solomon, of becoming so concerned for demonstrable security and stability that he felt impelled to make immediate arrangements for political and religious organisation – the pragmatic aim was peace. Once again, he had lacked the discipline to be reshaped by the Lord's greater agenda, which allows the focussing that gives identity, only as a basis for then having the courage and the confidence to reach out further, and find common ground in the grace which offers new life to all.

In our own roles, we can find ourselves in a similar place – the need to 'modernise' worship and encourage people to connect, and yet the danger of undermining the roots and core values of the gospel around which we are called to gather. Jeroboam could be a sign of new leadership in any parish – properly called and anointed, but tempted to make too comprehensive arrangements for worship and organisation, a desire to establish that peace and stability which is so important in human life. The danger is the temptation to avoid the disciplines of waiting, absorbing the incoherence of the cries of the human heart and shifting from being a mediator to becoming the leader who delivers through our own achievements.

But the prophet, who is such a necessary counterbalance to political and religious leadership, is by no means perfect or immune to temptation himself. Just as we can be tempted to judge politicians from the apparent security and superiority of the Gospel, so we should recognise that often we fail to be true to the good news of which we are agents.

The prophet had been told not to eat or drink with anybody in this foreign territory. He needed to be nourished from other sources (the fount/Jerusalem) and to be clear that he brought an outside perspective, not one meshed into the current thinking in the new kingdom. To be a prophet, he had to take seriously the need to be at a distance. This is the basis of the distinction between the pastoral and the prophetic.

He faces two temptations. Initially Jeroboam invites him to share table fellowship and receive gifts. This would have modelled reaching a compromise with a system he had been sent to challenge. Instead of leaving Jeroboam to reflect more deeply about this prophetic intervention, he would have given the King permission to believe that the warning had been heeded and a simple adjustment made by the destruction of the altar. This is the strategy of pastoral ministry, to hasten a sense of blessing. Sometimes, it is very appropriate. Occasionally it can serve to obscure the real call of God into a particular situation. To retreat and leave people to struggle takes courage – but it can be a vital part of the spiritual journey. The salt needs to sink in, not be washed away.

Secondly, temptation comes from another prophet. The old prophet lived at Bethel, so he had clearly made some kind of compromise with the new arrangements. He lies in saying that an angel had told him to invite the prophet from Judah. His lack of integrity as a prophet is illustrated by his emphasis that the angel spoke "to me" rather than to say that he had received the word of the Lord for others.

Are we more likely to be led astray by the earnestness of people within the ministry than by those from outside? Is there an empathy between leaders that can overcome inevitable competitiveness and create a temporary bond of false confidence in their own powers and projects?

The prophet is now tempted, not for pastoral reasons, but for religious reasons. The old prophet is a public minister, but inwardly he is corrupt. He has already compromised and he invites this younger prophet to compromise too. Once the younger man succumbs to the temptation, he is accused of hypocrisy and God's judgment is pronounced. Is this a sign of the deeper, underlying competitiveness amongst leaders? Is this the equivalent of political leaders fighting battles – but between prophetic leaders the conflict is more complex, nuanced, yet equally destructive of the integrity of all involved?

Prophecy faces temptation from the pastoral case for political compromise and the theological case made for religious compromise. Both invite the young prophet into "fellowship" that would undermine the distance that he needs to maintain if his credibility and effectiveness is to be preserved.

Both politics and religion tend to be conserving, and open to change only within what seems to be safe and manageable parameters. Prophecy brings a more radical challenge, the destruction of the very altars upon which human systems are constructed, and a call to a deeper conserving – that of God's revelation and declared way of working.

CHAPTER - 8

Formation for Prophetic Leadership
I Kings 17

The prophet from Judah was nameless. What was important was his office, not his person. His downfall was due to accepting a personal invitation, which drew him out of the role of his office, and therefore undermined his suitability to remain as a prophet of the Lord.

In Chapter seventeen, we begin to learn about the formation of a person, Elijah the Tishbite, to be a prophet, within a particular political context. In terms of the analogies we are exploring in this reading of I and II Kings, we have recognised something of the marks and temptations of the exercise of political (and religious) leadership through the stories of Solomon and other rulers. Now we are invited to consider the complementary role we are called to inhabit, of prophet, of the one anointed to challenge the inevitable temptations towards complacency and self-sufficiency and to invite leadership and discipleship to re-engage with the spiritual journey that enables the humility to make right choices and re-form arrangements appropriately.

Elijah the Tishbite. Prophecy is located, comes from and to particular places, but it is responsible for a bigger vision than any one place can easily perceive. The background is the rule of Ahab, who "did evil in the sight of the Lord more than all who were before him". The system of what we are identifying as 'political' leadership was becoming increasingly corrupt and self-centred – disconnected from God and His purposes. Ahab married Jezebel, who came from another political and religious culture – that of the Baals, with the erection of local altars and sacred poles to encourage an immediate access to blessing and guidance for people in their daily lives. It was successful because it scored highly in terms of pastoral effectiveness. People like immediate access to a means of negotiating their hopes and fears in a context that is domestic, comfortable and focussed upon the promotion of their own well-being. The therapy of multimedia communications could be seen as a modern equivalent! Ahab and Jezebel erected a system of signs and messages that localised spirituality and gave people the means of seeking peace, so that wider concerns were less significant. The pragmatic peacefulness pursued by political leadership. A system to win hearts and minds to quiescence. Today we call it political disengagement, leaving powerful factions to organise society as suits themselves best.

Elijah is called by God to announce a drought. We tend to think of a drought as a minor inconvenience – perhaps necessitating a hosepipe ban! In that part of the world, water is the key to life and its survival. Jesus bases much of His teaching on the importance of living water. Elijah is therefore saying that despite such a sophisticated system of political and religious organisation (echoes of Solomon), there will be no life or energy for the people. A key point to note is that because of this corrupt leadership, all the people will suffer. Leadership by definition is not simply about the leader – all for whom the leader is responsible suffer from poor performance. That is why leadership needs to be properly aligned to the purposes of God for all His children. Similarly the final judgment in Matthew 25 treats the people as ethne - in groups. We are inextricably connected: it is a myth to believe that anyone can operate or be judged simply as an individual. To be human is to be located in webs of relationships. Leadership takes responsibility for this reality. There can be no retreat into a smaller, more limited and more comfortable operation. Hence the concern about the corporate responsibility of business and the private sector.

In Elijah, we see the prophet being schooled in this particular form of leadership. First he calls attention to the bankruptcy of the self-sufficient world being established by Ahab and Jezebel. He does not offer an answer, or claim superior knowledge about more appropriate political and religious arrangements. He simply recognises the bankruptcy of these sophisticated systems of self-sufficiency. Next, Elijah retreats to the wilderness. God calls him not to the front line of continuing denunciation or alternative action. He is sent to the wilderness to receive a different perspective. This is how Jesus is formed for leadership too.

He withdraws to the Wadi Cherith – to a place where there is water: to a place where God can feed him. But then, the Wadi dries up. Instead of being given a stunning new vision and message through the discipline of something like a regular quiet day, the outcome of his withdrawal is to have to face the very bankruptcy that he sees society facing too. He is in no way superior or immune because he is being formed to be a prophet. His first experience of being drawn into a more spiritual discipline is not a sense of confidence and clarity, but a deeper confrontation with lack and limitation. He is as bankrupt as the political system he has criticized. Both share a real thirst, a confrontation with the fragility of human life, despite our best efforts, either politically (Ahab) or spiritually (Elijah). Prophet and politician are rooted in a common human frailty.

Then comes a word from the Lord, to go and live with a poor widow, who, with her son, is facing this bankruptcy of human capacities in its most extreme form. They are about to die. The widow is someone outside of, as at least on the edge of, the normal safe systems devised by political and religious organisation. This was still true in the time of Jesus and Paul. These two people, the widow and her son, were alone, collecting sticks and starving. Everyone suffered from the drought. Elijah had faced his own spiritual and the physical bankruptcy. Now he is to join others in a similar plight.

Amazingly, the woman receives him into her household. A powerful sign of Eastern hospitality to the stranger, whatever the circumstances. In adversity, two strangers can combine to form a new household. In the west, we would do a risk assessment and close the door to Elijah! In this context, strangers are drawn together as the basic means of life are disappearing.

Elijah says 'do not be afraid'. He encourages the woman to risk, to have faith in the potential of this new fellowship that God is creating. He asks her to share her limited resources with the stranger. The woman has her own plans: she abandons them and gives priority to loving the stranger in need. The result, like the Feeding of the Five Thousand, is a miracle of multiplication. The nourishment keeps coming: the meal and oil do not run out. Meal and oil, of course, are bread and wine.

Here the prophet begins to offer a positive response to the crisis of bankruptcy. Not a bright new plan. Rather a new household is formed – one that we can recognise as a Eucharistic community – strangers surviving and thriving together through the sharing of bread and wine – provided by the grace of God as the source of new life and new relationships. This miracle is not providing a new politics or economics, but it offers sustenance and new life, which can become the energy of a new politics. The Eucharistic community remains small, fragile, dependent upon God's continuing formation. It is a sign not a solution: a sacrament, not a system to be simply exported. It operates on the boundary between life and death, and the miraculous gift of new life. It emerges from a faithful dependence upon the mercy and power of God to sustain and bless life in all its fragility. This Eucharistic community is most easily understood and inhabited by the poor and the prophet.

Elijah's further formation as a prophet emerges from the final part of the narrative. Just as the new household, the Eucharistic community seems to be providing salvation, the son of the Household dies. The son has been silent and insignificant, yet present in the community. Now he is to be the one who helps the members discern its proper meaning and purpose.

The son enacts the vulnerability and the mortality of the community. The breath leaves him. Immediately the woman interprets his death as punishment for her sin. Death is the enemy, a judgment on fallen humanness – such is the deep instinct in the soul for immortality and eternity. In fact the Eucharistic community is for sinners; the bankrupt, the dying.

Prophecy is not about finding out sin and pronouncing judgment. All are sinners, including the prophet. Elijah takes the son to an upper room (an echo of the Last Supper, where the role of the Son is interpreted and offered as the key to new life). He prays to God and stretches himself out on the child three times. Three is a number of completeness. The outcome of this act of trust and worship and the crying of the human heart for new life – is that the listening heart of God responds with an act of resurrection. The son, who was dead, killed by the bankruptcy brought by the political and religious systems, and the breath of God which had departed from this key person in the Eucharistic community, are restored to new life. The son is raised from the dead into the Eucharistic community, to teach it something about the power and purpose of God in its midst, a sign and an invitation to others too. "See your son is alive" is the message of the prophet, against all the odds. There has been no change in the political and economic context – but there is a sign and a word – a theology – that the prophet has experienced himself, amidst the poorest of the poor. This sign and word is the key to the good news the prophet is raised up to offer. This is the core of the task of prophetic leadership.

The woman, like Mary the first apostle of this sign of the resurrection of the son, confirms his vocation: "Now I know that you are a man of God and that the word of the Lord in your mouth is truth"

In a sense, this woman ordains Elijah to be a prophet, now formed and established in role. 'You are a man of God; the word in your mouth is truth': He is a minister of sacrament and word and she ordains him to the vocation to be a prophet

– a leader of God's people amidst the frailty and bankruptcy of human being.

Elijah is formed as a prophet by being set apart, perceiving the bankruptcy of political and religious arrangements disconnected from God's greater purposes, facing his own limitations, engaging with the poorest to establish a Eucharistic community of total dependency on God's grace, recognising the sign of the son raised from the dead, bringer of new life against the odds, into the mayhem of everyday life and then ordained by a woman who had been privileged to share in and witness this journey and the grace that can issue through it.

CHAPTER - 9

True and False Prophets

I Kings 18

The chapter starts with the phrase 'in the third year'. In scripture, the notion of the third is code for an important moment, a gift of new life and resurrection. There had been a long drought – a sustained demonstration of the limitation to human life without God's grace and mercy. Much seems uneven and beyond the control of even the most sophisticated systems. The prophet Elijah is called to announce the arrival of rain, a salvation to a decaying society.

He confronts a system which is still conducting its own search for water, for life. Obadiah is a spiritual person working in this corrupt political and religious system. At one level he conforms to public expectations about belief and behaviour designed to promote growth and welfare, but in another sense, in his inner life and in more private actions, he is trying to preserve the place of prophecy in an organisation which sees no need for it. Many Christians could identify with this double life. The witness of a disciple in a corrupt system is one of great complexity and challenge. It often seeks the support of prophetic leadership, rather than the pastoral care that might be more readily available. Most of us live in a culture that can call for some kind of compromise about our faith, in terms of public life. Elijah the prophet is going to challenge this disciple to risk more and not simply be shaped by a worldly desire for peace and security. These latter qualities easily became goals for Christians in our own times, especially in our public intercessions.

The prophetic leader needs to ask whether or not such an apparently attractive spirituality is in fact serving to obscure a failing of proper witness.

Having challenged Obadiah, the disciple, to risk more for the sake of the Kingdom, Elijah then confronts Ahab. A direct clash between the political system and the prophetic word of God. "You have forsaken the commandments of the Lord" the challenge of the 'if' to provoke deeper reflection, 'you have followed the Baals', i.e. you have established a more flexible, domestic and easily accessible system of seeking blessing for individuals and small groups on their own terms – and not as part of a more universal dynamic.

Elijah accepts that political systems have their own prophets. No one can ignore the importance of signs and slogans to give shape and direction to the hearts and minds of the people. The New Labour government was famous for a prophetic streak which pronounced 'we don't do God' – there were more immediate dynamics to keep in focus if political organisation was to be successful. Governments need to invent some kind of theology and 'religion', even if it is reduced to the catchphrase 'we don't do God'! The prophet of the Lord is called to confront these lesser, more limited theologies and their prophets.

But, Elijah also confronts the people – those subject to leadership. How long will they go limping with two different opinions? This is a typically prophetic statement – a graphic image. Limping means that they could not walk properly or proceed smoothly.

They had too many ideas and views; they were confused and paralysed by the plethora of options. Freedom to believe and behave under the banner of the Baals created confusion and paralysis – a pliable people for a powerful leadership. There is a subtle art of encouraging variety so as to induce more direct dependence upon the mechanisms needed to create a holding framework. The pragmatic god of peace and stability becomes the one common focus for the confusing range of options that people are enabled to develop. The people limp and thus need the support of the state: or of the church: both offer opportunities for strong leadership.

The prophet of the Lord begins this demonstration of prophetic leadership by confronting the political leaders and the people: both must be challenged. One for a simplistic system focussed on selfish need, the other for occupying that space with a limping diversity. The odds seem overwhelming (as they would be in good Eastern storytelling). There are 450 prophets of Baal and only Elijah. Jesus often spoke of leaven and salt. This should be normative proportions for prophetic leadership, in challenging planning that is based upon risk assessment or observing successful ways of promoting religion in a particular society.

The confrontation that the prophet creates is around the sacrifice of bulls. This is confronting the political system on its own terms. The influence of Egypt made the worship of bulls very important, and Jeroboam had erected two Golden Calves as an indication of this fact. Aaron had similarly been tempted to produce a Golden Calf. The people were limping between two opinions or pathways. The prophet was going to point to a clear choice that could be made, between their heritage which continued to give some shape to the worship of the people, and their present preferences for the priests and prophets of the Baals – for a more domestic and self-centred spirituality.

The means of confrontation is not political debate, nor the demonstration of growth and welfare. The confrontation is enacted through public worship and ritual. Elijah consults public opinion and the people agree to this form of trial. Ordinary people recognise that public ritual is one of the few ways in which common space and unrestricted participation can be offered. Public ritual, like royal weddings, enables a huge variety of engagements of hearts and minds, without the refining and restrictive interpretation and control of political systems of organisation.

The appeal is to God – or the gods – by fire, by the testing, purifying power of Divine purposes, which destroy the old in order to create new life: the key is the offering of the people into this process.

The prophets of Baal go through the routines and display the signs through which they offer confirmation and support to the existing arrangement. Their rituals include the shedding of blood, their own blood. Significantly, as they perform this task of public leadership, they 'limp' about the altar – they too have no clear movement or direction, they are somehow incapacitated from delivering what is the basis of their religion – more instant access to the presence and power of God, focussed to meet the particular context and occasion. There is no response.

When it comes to Elijah's turn, he does two things. First he insists upon giving God a more direct role – calling upon the Lord to be present. Second, he insists upon giving the people a more direct role, he calls them to come closer. The prophet places himself as a mediator between God and His people.

Next he repairs the altar of the Lord, which has been destroyed to make way for a more modern, flexible approach to worship, based upon toleration, diversity and speedy access.

He takes 12 stones, an echo of Moses in Exodus 24. There is a tradition, a priority to the completeness of God's concern, the inclusivity of every tribe to be equally represented. There is an inherited way of worship: the 12 stones signify the whole people of God being present in the liturgy – whether physically proximate or not. This is not an occasion for easy access on the terms of those who choose to use this particular approach to God. In public worship, God visits and renews His covenant with all His people. A key part of prophetic leadership is to invite people to engage with what God has already done – drawing closer to His power and presence, even by turning towards His altar in prayer.

When Elijah digs the trench for the water to be poured over the sacrifice, we see a dramatic enacting of the distance between what sensible human systems would design to be effective and efficient, and the way in which God actually works to transform our imperfection into the stuff at His Kingdom. The fire will not come until the ludicrous bankruptcy of human plans and analysis has been fully exposed.

The ritual happens "at the time of the offering of the oblation." It is not a spectacular one-off event. Prophetic leadership operates within the established rhythm and doctrine of God's forming of His people through regular public worship – rooted in re-membrance, reflection and resurrection. God has established this rhythm for His people to regularly seek His guidance; it provides the basis of the spiritual journey that each is invited to walk. Thus he offers a prayer to Abraham, Isaac and Jacob – he uses established liturgical language. The whole event is presented as part of the normal relationship between God and His people.

He knows his own place as a prophet "I am your servant." He has done all these things at God's bidding. The prophet is faithful to the Lord, not a wild innovator. He prays that God may answer so that the people's hearts may 'be turned back.' A picture of the dedication of the Temple and the invitation to every heart to turn and cry out to the listening heart of God.

The fire falls and consumes the offering, the altar, the water. Just as the fire of crucifixion fell and consumed Jesus – so as to turn hearts and release the gift of new life. Christians still consume the body of Jesus, to turn our hearts and receive the gift of new life. The prophet knows about the power of God's presence, consuming all that we offer, consuming ourselves in our owning our frailty and weakness, and turning our hearts into agents of new life. So the people fall on their faces in worship. They turn their hearts to the Lord.

Elijah then destroys the false prophets. The prophet imitates the ways of the world far too easily, especially when he strays from standing at a distance, on the edge, being the mediator, to becoming an implementor, a politician, a producer of practical plans. Elijah will be given a further lesson with regard to this temptation.

Having exercised this prophetic leadership in such a public way, he goes to the top of the mountain, as Moses did after dealing with the apostasy of the Golden Calf. Moses ascended the mountain to seek God's mercy and guidance for his people. Elijah goes to the mountain and bows down: he himself worships. He too must practice this dependency on the spiritual journey, as he had just challenged others to observe. He needs to wait, observe, seek the signs. He sees a small cloud – of no significance to human calculations. As a prophet, Elijah knows that a small amount is enough. A sign brings salvation.

Finally, and movingly, Elijah then leads Ahab as he returns to the city in order to taste God's salvation for himself. Elijah does not judge this terrible King, he simply leads him towards the place where new life will be given. The power of God does not bring clarity of analysis or assessment – but it does bring gracious new life to all, wicked and good alike. The field remains a mix of wheat and tares after the exercise of prophetic leadership, as it was before.

CHAPTER - 10

The Renewal of Prophetic Leadership
I Kings 19

S amuel had warned the people of God about the oppressive tendencies of Kingship. Ahab and Jezebel had magnified these temptations into a complete system of political and religious control. Elijah had been raised up as a 'prophet of the Lord' to confront this bankrupt idolatry and had exterminated all the prophets of the Baals, the shapers of personal and corporate spirituality for their people. Ahab and Jezebel react to this challenge with hostility, even though the prophet's intervention had brought salvation and new life in the form of water to relieve the drought. They remained committed to a system under their own control.

Elijah stood alone against the political and religious organisation of his people. The testing ground was not based on an audit of institutional arrangements and performance, it was worship at the altar of sacrifice. This is where prophecy operates and from where re-formation by the forgiveness and grace of God flows to those who would receive it. This courageous stand became the model for all prophetic leadership. Elijah is mentioned in the Gospel of Matthew, in the letter of James, in relation to John the Baptist, he is one of the key figures at the Transfiguration when Jesus is seen most clearly in His glory – His power and His purpose. Elijah was rooted in true liturgy, which offers cleansing and renewal to all the people. But the established powers react with hostility – conflict continues, as we should expect from worship focussed on the reality of sacrifice.

Again the forces of the system are ranged against Elijah. He was afraid and fled for his life. There needs to be a certain pragmatism and self-protection in the prophet's armoury: he cannot simply stand alone and expect God to vanquish his enemies. Elijah has already learned that God manifests His power not to destroy His enemies, but to turn their hearts and to offer the blessing of salvation through the gift of the water of new life. This gracious generosity puts the prophet's life at risk.

Once more he retreats into the wilderness. He cries out from his own heart – he is exhausted, dispirited and disappointed. An angel comes to sustain him. God's miraculous presence and care continue, even in the depths of this despair. In his exhaustion, God makes him eat and sleep: eat and sleep. He continues to advance into the wilderness, to Mount Horeb, where Moses had met God.

How often is our own exercise of leadership a dynamic between moments of obvious blessing and 'success' and the reality of continuing problems, pressure, opposition? Such a confusing and challenging dynamic can easily lead to the self-pity and depression that Elijah seems to experience. Yet, rather than a theological analysis of his experience, Elijah simply goes further into the wilderness, pushing himself more and more on to nothing but the mercy of God. He owns all his sense of failure and frustration and seeks no immediate remedy – either for his personal circumstances or for his public role. He simply waits in the place of emptiness, owning his own need and inadequacy. He simply allows his heart to cry out. And in this distressed state, with no medication or doctor's note!, in God's time, there is a response. 'The word of the Lord came to him' Not with an answer, but with a question – 'what are you doing here?' He is to be guided even further into an honest exploration of his journey, his motives, his interpretation. Having articulated his own understanding of his story, Elijah is still not given comfort or an answer; he is told to 'stand on the mountain before the Lord'. At the very moment when he displays the classic signs of what we call stress, feeling isolated, with no support – he is forced to acknowledge the reality of such a situation. There is no rush to provide pastoral care and comfort. The prophet is called to stand alone in the place of challenge – with no vision, no comfort, no support. The prophet incarnates the fact that none of us can live in a state of perpetual blessing. We need to face the ups and the downs and be prepared to be renewed through darkness and despair, as much as through the experience of blessing and achievement.

Then comes the famous passage about the wind, the earthquake and the fire. All classical images of God's power and presence, as is well attested in Scripture. But for the prophet, the guardian of this precious and formative inheritance, God is not revealed in these spectacular places – he is known in the still-small voice – in the silence of a heart crying out for salvation. This is a deeper, more personal encounter – sometimes translated as 'sheer silence.' The paradox that in what is apparently no communication, the deepest and clearest communication can take place. Classical spirituality teaches that God is met most profoundly in the nothingness. God is there all along – beneath his litany of complaint and depression, beneath the storms of the world, beneath the narrative of oppression and threat. Elijah has had to retreat deep into the wilderness to hear this voice. Prophetic leadership must be rooted and continually renewed through this process of retreat, honest owning of frustrations and failings and paying attention to hear the response from the listening heart of God.

After this precious moment to renew his call to be a prophet of the Lord, Elijah remains the same person, with the same problems and the same lament! He is not suddenly transformed into a happy, fully confident representative minister of the good news. He remains unsure, hesitant, still feeling alone and threatened.

What is different after this encounter which renews his prophetic leadership is that he can discern more clearly what God wants him to do. 'Go, return, anoint Hazael, anoint Jehu'. He is to identify and encourage a new generation of political leaders. God remains faithful to His covenant with His people and continually forgives and renews their political and religious life. New kings are to be called for Aram and for Israel. The prophet is to be faithful to this persistence of grace and goodness, even against all the odds in terms of measurable evidence.

The Prophet is called to identify and bless other vocations, his own role remains peripheral – at a distance – in terms of the organisation of day to day affairs. It is never easy for those of us in leadership roles to recognise and accept the limitations on our own roles and responsibilities. Such discernment and discipline is vital if the people of God are to flourish and be led by the range of gifts God can raise up – each called amidst the temptations to short term security and self-centred glorification.

Lastly, just as Elijah is renewed in his prophetic leadership, he is instructed to appoint a successor. Most of us would find such a challenge very threatening! 'Anoint Elisha prophet in your place'! Tenure of office is limited. It is not a personal possession, but a public role, called, commissioned and continually renewed by God.

There will come a moment when, for God's purposes, there needs to be renewal through the appointment of a new person "in your place". Few of us would welcome such a stark statement of what we know to be inevitable.

As we know, Elisha becomes a prophet who did twice as many miracles as Elijah and who inherits a double portion of his spirit. How readily do we look around us for more able successors 'to take our place'?

It is interesting to note the process of making such an appointment. Elisha separates himself from his family and his livelihood. He is asked to be formed through an apprenticeship model, rather than by attending one of the schools of the prophets. In our terms, he is formed in the parish rather than through a college or course. The formation operates through a collaborative approach, emerging from his willing sacrifice of his previous vocation. To be a prophet is to be set apart – placed at a distance: by a process of renewal.

CHAPTER - 11

The Renewal of Political Leadership

I Kings 21

The story of Ahab and Naboth exposes the dynamic between ruler and ruled: king and subject, Ahab has established a complete system of political and religious organisation, giving space for localised spirituality, within the wider frame of the requirements of the kingdom. But beneath such apparently sensible and reasonable arrangements, there is always the potential for conflict and dispute.

The narrative hinges on two phrases. 'Vineyard' in scripture is a metaphor for God's enterprise, especially in the teaching of Jesus. It describes the workings of creation, the relationship of Creator to creatures and the challenges of ensuring a proper fruitfulness. The vineyard is an image of God's life pouring into the material of creation to give life. Naboth the citizen knew about this image and about this reality. He owned a vineyard.

In the same sentence comes the phrase 'vegetable garden' The word thus translated only appears in one other place in scripture – in Deuteronomy 11,[10] where the land of Egypt is referred to as a 'vegetable garden'.

Therefore the chapter revolves around two key images. The vineyard – sign of God's presence amongst His people and of how He orders life. And the vegetable garden – sign of the human civilisation of which Egypt was the great model at that time. The word refers to a vegetable garden that is irrigated in a particular way, through human ingenuity.

The conflict between Ahab and Naboth is a clash between a political ruler who desires to develop up to date modern methods of organisation and a religious citizen, who is resistant to this mark of progress, because of a prior loyalty to the way God has entrusted this part of His vineyard to Naboth's family. A clash of two civilisations: the religious civilisation of the vineyard and the Egyptian civilisation of the vegetable garden. Tradition challenged by progress.

Ahab is engaged in what we can recognise as territorial consolidation. It makes sense to extend his property in developing this particular style of vegetable garden. Naboth seems to be an irritating, old fashioned person, locked into an ancient and out-of-date religious view of the world. He believes that because God has given the vineyard to his family, they cannot let go of this stewardship that has been allocated to them.

As a reasonable, enlightened, modern ruler, Ahab offers a fair exchange. We live in a world where fairness is the basis of common values and common life. Fairness often seems like the ultimate value. We worship the god of toleration –

everything is allowable as long as it is fair. Ahab offers an exchange of land, or money for the value of the land – how can anybody resist such a fair offer?

But Naboth is bound by a religious law. God has given this land to his family and it is part of their vocation to be stewards of it. The land is not theirs to trade: it is God's. They cannot let it go; the law of religion forbids it.

We are all too familiar with this type of clash- between political fairness and what appears to be religious bigotry. The political seems to be rational and fair: religion seems to be uneven, mysterious, incomprehensible – it gets in the way of progress.

Ahab is so convinced of his case, that when he is refused, he becomes angry and then depressed. His role is to lead the people into a new future: the key is to march with progress. He wants to promote 'Egyptification' – proven models of progress to advance the quality of life and the better management of resources. Growth and welfare require this kind of development if they are to be sustained.

However, the king respects the religious stance of Naboth. He does not insist upon the process of Egyptification at all costs. He is frustrated and annoyed, but handles these responses as many of us do in complex situations, by internalising them. He takes no public action, but he goes home and sulks: just as we might do after a difficult PCC meeting!

His wife Jezebel has to endure the sulk and challenges him not to give up on their project of modernisation. She says that he should not be depressed by religion that is so out of touch, rather she will organise decisive action.

In fact, what she is saying is that in order for their political and religious project to continue to flourish on the terms they have designed – it is better for one man to die, for all the people to therefore flourish. The vineyard is often a site of the deepest Gospel message.

Letters are sealed and sent, an echo of David and Uriah the Hittite. This use of political power is exercised, ironically, through a religious festival. Politics and religion need to be closely aligned if a pragmatic peace is to prevail. This is the common ground on which political and religious leaders continue to meet.

One of the key tools for holding people together is public ritual and festival. This is often the source of public identity and an acting out of fuller connectivity: notwithstanding that such rituals and festivals are generally managed by small groups for their own interests. Hence the political investment in the 2012 Olympics in the UK.

Church life uses a similar approach to festivals and occasions of encounter to encourage a greater sense of connection and common purpose. Sometimes, these methods of outreach can offer an uncritical endorsement of political values, thereby avoiding any consideration of a more prophetic challenge or critique. If occasions of public connection endorse small interest groups and obscure issues of justice and oppression, then there may be a case for a more careful consideration of how to pursue the invitation to Porch and Assembly, in a climate where these places can seem mere examples of all kinds of similar processes.

Naboth is accused of cursing God and the King. Not a dissimilar charge to that put to Jesus – 'are you the Messiah?

Are you a King?' Religion and politics dislike any outside claims or wider perspective. Progress needs to be managed and carefully controlled. Naboth is found guilty, on the evidence of false witnesses. This innocent man is taken outside of the city and stoned. This is a powerful way in which Egyptification, our modernisation, handles religion, by seeking to bury it, as Naboth would have been buried under a heap of stones. Religion is put in a tomb – as happened in the Garden with the body of Jesus.

In the nineteenth century terminology coined by Nietzsche 'God is dead' – religion is buried. Ahab can continue his project of sensible modernisation. Science will run the world, not religion. Rationalism will be the tool, not tradition and ancient ritual. Egyptification is the answer to the needs of humanity – increase irrigation and people will be fed from an efficient vegetable garden – something more predictable and profitable than the laborious tending of ancient vines.

Then – the word of the Lord comes to Elijah. Such political corruption must be challenged. The prophet is summoned. The task of the prophet is not to offer a critique of the vegetable garden scheme, nor to comment more generally on the project of modernization. Progress need not be incompatible with religion. Yet Ahab immediately recognises the prophet as his 'enemy'. There is a deep clash between the way in which political leadership is operating and God's call for common ground to be found, not in modernising progress (the myth of globalisation) but in a mutual sense of humility, dependence upon God and the gift of His new life.

Elijah, who presumably was accompanied by his apprentice Elisha, pronounces a fearsome judgment – another act of cleansing and opportunity for renewal for all the people, by the raising up of new leadership.

Perhaps the most challenging moment for the prophet comes in the final verses, when Ahab repents. He humbles himself and turned towards the Lord. He owned his failings, his limitations and his needs. Once again, prophetic leadership does not provide an answer, but simply calls for the renewal of the political and religious system. Even this terrible King ('there was no-one like Ahab, who sold himself to do evil') could hear something positive from the prophet and repent.

How often does our engagement with prophetic leadership draw us into a self-righteousness that not only proclaims God's judgment, but also expects systems to change and become more perfect. There is an enormous challenge in having to articulate to call to be renewed and then witness the most unlikely and apparently undeserving people receive the blessing. Prophecy is rooted in the encounter of the inner person with God.

Elijah had learned this through the still small voice. This mystery and grace needs to be extended to others. External standards and behaviours are not an accurate sign of the life of the soul – the sheer complexity and mystery of the inner workings of human being. There is a priestly element to prophetic leadership in a society that is always seeking Egyptification – a wisdom to somehow give space for God's grace to meet people and effect a change, which needs to be noticed, respected and hallowed – even if the outward systems seem to be largely unaffected. Wisdom expressed by Jesus in the parable of the publican and the Pharisee.

Through one act of repentance, Ahab is saved. The system remains under judgment. Such generosity seems beyond all reason: he has been involved in the murder of an innocent man in an attempt to crush religion. But the prophet must recognise the depth of God's mercy, just as Jesus calls for us to love our enemies. No logic: just love. No sort out: just new life – renewal.

CHAPTER - 12

Power and Prayer

II Kings 2

The predominant model of leadership tends to be the political, often allied to the religious. This can make for the effective oversight and organisation of society. But the stronger the systems that are developed and the more deeply entrenched powerful interest groups become, the less space is available for new life and the re-formation that brings renewal. Hence the undermining of such establishments from the forces of inward insensitivity and external rivalry.

In this new book of Kings, we see the successful continuation of Ahab's line through his son Ahaziah and then its survival through the latter's brother. Ahaziah faces two pressure points. Moab rebelled against Israel, and the King injured himself through a fall, and thus lay injured. Both pressures threatened his security and it was in order to remain in control of the situation, that he sends messages to inquire of the God of Ekron, Baal-zebub, whether or not he will recover.

In contrast to this passing of power from one person to another only through the death of the officeholder, Elijah has already recruited Elisha to accompany him as a means of enabling a different kind of succession – based upon the call of God to an unexpected individual, rather than as the result of a particular group intent on remaining in control. The political succession of Ahaziah contrasts with the vocational succession already in train as Elisha is formed through his accompanying apprenticeship. Prophetic leadership issues from a specific call, not through hereditary and group processes. It is important in our own appointments to leadership roles amongst God's people, that the forces of traditional expectations and group interests do not provide such strong shaping that the call of God to an hitherto unknown person cannot be recognised and accepted. For us, the dual roles of political and prophetic leadership make processes of succession and appointment particularly complex because of this inevitable tension between the political importance of continuity and stability, alongside the prophetic role that always emerges unexpectedly and highlighting critical possibilities for new life.

In terms of the modelling of political leadership, Ahaziah, the leader responsible for security, has had an accident. No system or structure can prevent accidents, despite the contemporary mantra which seems to accompany every disaster – 'we will take steps to make sure this never happens again'.

The King has had a fall. Christians know that to fall is part of the human condition, but there is little expectation that political systems will fall. They are designed to do the opposite.

Of course political arrangements do fall – but generally the expectation tries to deny that possibility.

Political and their allied religious systems tend to assume that their arrangements are normative. Churches often operate on similar assumptions. This helps to explain why the King is so concerned and seeks guidance about his future – for he embodies the organisation over which he presides.

He asks his messengers to consult the god of Ekron, which was a Philistine settlement. It had a history of being occupied by Israel and then reclaimed by the Philistines. The territory experienced the fragility of political and religious organisation that could fall and be superseded. Ahaziah had asked his advisors where he could look for the best advice and they pointed him towards Baal-zebub, god of Ekron.

. The angel of the Lord tells Elijah to intercept these messengers and to offer different advice. The careful calculations of the political are challenged by one who stands outside of this world, at a distance – and is thus able to hear other voices than the immediate conversation so characteristic of politics – 'here is a problem – what is the answer?' Prophetic leadership is called out from different, deeper, more mysterious sources, and is charged to intercept and challenge this uncritical worship of the gods of the day. Baal-zebub must have given evidences to contemporaries of some effectiveness and this had been duly noted by the King's advisers and the information produced to steer policy at the appropriate time. There needs to be an outside voice, a wider perspective, if politics is to be renewed and its leadership properly advised – even if the advice was as devastating as a sentence to death.

It may have been the fact that Baal-zebub was known for giving more hopeful advice and direction that encouraged the royal advisers to suggest this consultation.

Once Ahaziah realises that it is the prophet Elijah who has intervened and offered such a gloomy message, the King desires him to come and see him, no doubt hoping for a more merciful judgment.

Elijah has told him that there is a God in Israel. This reminds him that God is closer to him than he thinks, ready to hear the cries of the heart (as had been the case with Ahab). Secondly, Elijah reminds the King that the spiritual journey involves a choice. God gives human beings a radical freedom to choose – either to trust themselves to Him or to seek other systems and supports – more localised gods.

Ahaziah works differently. His sending of a cohort of fifty men to invite Elijah to come down to him indicates that in fact he offered no choice. Political leadership cannot afford to offer much in the way of choice – it works best by inducing conformity (even through a popular mechanism such as occasional elections in our own case). It is this temptation to control, for the sake of a pragmatic peacefulness, providing a firm frame to hold more personal and local 'choices', which is the hallmark of what often appears to be successful political leadership.

By contrast, Elijah represents a God who works through a covenant that offers his faithful commitment alongside a radical freedom to accept or ignore this offer. Many of us oscillate between the two possibilities – and thus shift from the new life of renewal to the stubbornness of working to our own script and priorities. This almost inevitable oscillation in a personal spiritual journey is much less easy to allow in a political or religious organisation, because the commonly worshipped god of peace and stability cannot cope with such unevenness and turbulence.

Once again, we are presented with two models of leadership. Ahaziah is the political leader seeking contemporary wisdom in order to maintain progress or growth amidst stability and adequate welfare. Elijah the prophetic leader looks at this world from a distance, from outside, and interprets it not through the lense of present and desired future, but through a tradition and a mystery that requires mediation and a prayerful attention. Human fallenness is too persistent for any kind of 'cure' beyond entering the rhythm of heart calling to the listening heart of God for forgiveness and new life.

Similarly, there are contrasting sources of wisdom for each of these models of leadership. Baal-zebub is a term used only in this passage in II Kings in the Old Testament. But it is a term used by Jesus on a number of occasions in the New Testament. In the Gospel Jesus exercises power not as Baal-zebub, a localised, popular god for a particular group or place. Rather, Jesus exercises power because God comes down to deal with false gods – as fire from heaven. By contrast, Ahaziah sends a captain and fifty men – a much more localised and direct form of power. Elijah calls down fire from heaven and this human expression of power is destroyed. Just as political power which is usually sustained in this manner will eventually fall and be consumed. God's greater agenda consumes the pettiness of politics. This happens twice, to make the point absolutely clear.

The contest is between the political, which is power, and prayer, which is petitioning.

The King gives orders which are obeyed. Elijah hinges his prayer of response on that key word which shapes the true spiritual journey – 'if'. 'If I am a man of God'......'if' he is in proper dependent, humble relationship with God then the cry of his heart will be heard and the power of politics can be overridden.

Power and prayer are different routes for the exercise of leadership. Others look to leaders to manifest power, often this is the key to any credibility – but this can only be demonstrated against measurable human criteria: the effectiveness of systems that produce the pragmatic peace. By contrast, prayer places the situation in a totally different and dependent frame, where the timing and the outcomes are in God's gift and they are often unexpected and challenging to what has been established as 'normal'. It is very difficult to be a prayerful leader in a world where the predominant models are exemplified by the captain and his fifty.

The task of the parish priest, as both political and prophetic leader, has to pay special attention to the demands for effective outcomes and the place of prayer, reflection, waiting, retreating to the wilderness, and receiving insights that challenge the maintenance of the status quo for the sake of renewal.

The third captain of 50 exhibits a different approach. Not the direct demand to conform to naked power. Rather, he comes humbly, with a petition, a prayer for mercy. He offers the cry of his heart, not a curt command. This is the person to whom Elijah can relate. They go together to the King – two prayerful people. The political representative and the prophet can stand on common ground when there is a mutuality rooted in humility, prayerfulness and owning the cry of the heart. This models the creative connection that is possible between the two kinds of leadership. Similarly, there are Kings of Israel who attain to this close and creative collaboration with the prophets of the Lord. There does not have to be rivalry and conflict between the two offices – there can be co-operation and a common journeying together.

Elijah tells the King that he will die. This kind of narrow leadership and focus on local gods is mortal. Yet the passage ends with the acts of Ahaziah being recorded for posterity. It is easier to appreciate bad leadership which is strong and strident, rather than prayerful, gentle, gracious leadership that may act invisibly like salt, as much as demonstrably in the public arena.

The leadership exercised by Elijah emerges from worship, prayerfulness, which is open to the larger, outside perspective and shaping of God. Too easily the leadership we exercise in our churches can place this genuine prayerfulness within systems of organisation and structures of worship, so that the space for a distant, critical, revelatory word is closed down. The kenosis of God is the willingness to withdraw in order to create space for others. This remains the most challenging aspect of leadership in any mode. There is an important hiddenness belonging to our God, who therefore beckons us to follow Him on a journey, paying attention to the still small voice and being prepared to be surprised and changed by His constant offer of new life. It is the tradition, the remembering and the signs or sacraments that He provides, which enable us to trust Him through hiddenness and apparent absence, and to recognise and rejoice in His presence. Those who hold the word of remembering and the sacraments of enacting are the people called to what we have been able to recognise of prophetic leadership.

As Ahaziah falls, Elijah goes up to the top of the mountain. The prophet retreats into the wilderness in order to invite those inhabiting civilised settlements on the plain to come up higher – to meet the word of the Lord at a distance from domestic security.

For a king too ill to move who asks him to 'come down', the prophet descends, but only to bring the fire of judgment, the challenging perspective that the mountain provides upon a sheltering gathering world.

Prophetic leadership needs to understand and inhabit this dynamic. It is the clue to recognising and receiving the gifts that God offers. How does our worship enable a similar experience to other disciples too? This is the spiritual process of atonement; raised up to the place of fire, the cross, to be sent down to engage others in this life restoring process. The third captain experienced this gift.

CHAPTER - 13

Continuity and Change
II Kings 2

The succession of political leadership is important for stability and is often handed (or wrestled) from one power group to another. We see this with the succession of kings in these texts. By contrast, the succession in prophetic leadership occurs as a response to God's call and is rooted in an important continuity - 'the word of the Lord', In the case of Elijah and Elisha, there has been a period of overlap and apprenticeship. Elisha has been formed in the prophetic tradition prior to his authorisation. Prophetic leadership is located in continuity, yet called to bring challenge and change. Most of us feel more comfortable in one of these modes; it calls for particular gifts and skills to be able to inhabit both – not least because disciples often divide into similar camps, between those who seek stability and those who seek something new. It is not enough for us to make our contribution and leave, there is an important responsibility upon everyone in a church to take seriously the importance of succession planning and management, while being open to the surprises of new people and new ways.

Each of us stands in a succession, and sometimes that can be oppressive, since there is often a tendency to measure the present against an imagined 'golden past'. Another pressure can be the expectation of handing on from our own stewardship so that nothing has been lost, and important advances are secured. In fact, neither of these factors, continuity and change, should be determinative of prophetic leadership. They simply provide part of the context within which the prophet invites hearts to turn to the Lord and be open to renewal. The key continuity is that of being open to receive grace, salvation and hope. And our consolation is the knowledge that the contribution of any leader is only part of a much richer mosaic.

In this chapter, we observe Elijah rounding off his ministry of prophetic leadership, and Elisha being confirmed and authorised as his successor. The transition involves Elijah visiting a number of key communities, and Elisha being seen to share in this journey and then to be tested in terms of his own sense of call.

Elisha displays total loyalty to his master. 'I will not leave you' He is offered the chance to stay behind when Elijah makes his farewell progression, but he is committed to being part of the spiritual journey through which prophetic leadership is formed and defined. He is ready to enter the difficult territory of offering challenge which may not be appreciated or understood and yet, which seeks to be articulated and enacted.

The ministry of prophetic leadership emerges from movement. Journeying from place to place maintains the possibility of seeing from different perspectives and helps to safeguard against a comfortable domestication of the 'word of the Lord' or its possible implications. Jesus and Paul are both constantly on the move, and it is often on the road, in between the settled spaces, that new light can shine – most classically for Paul on the way to Damascus: more regularly for Jesus in His daily withdrawing a distance to go apart and pray.

Elijah is sent to Bethel and then to Jericho. In each place, there is a 'company of prophets'. This was a school for the formation of prophets and for the nourishment of their ministries. There was a college in each place, where people were trained for the spiritual journey from which prophetic leadership emerged. Elijah was probably known to these communities of formation, perhaps as some form of visiting lecturer.

Interestingly, Elisha had not been trained in the school of the prophets. He had been trained through a contextual method – the model of apprenticeship. The dialogue hints that the self-consciously highly trained 'graduate' type prophets were rather snooty about Elisha. They came and said to him 'do you know that today the Lord will take your master away from you? He replied 'I do, keep silent' (or shut up!) Two types of pedagogy easily give rise to different evaluations of training and competence. This is not unknown in the church. The critical edge of those formed in the academic community of the company of the prophets implies that they know more than Elisha. His reply displays a certain amount of irritation!

The company of prophets knew that Elijah was to be taken away, but they had no idea of how, or the significance of such an event, or the implications for succession in prophetic leadership. Their insight and evaluation was based upon a rather static perspective, assuming that changes would be within an existing framework. Such a viewpoint was almost inevitable for those formed in a place, a centre of excellence confident in its own strengths and identity.

These exchanges also illustrate the tendency within any institutionalised structure of leadership for issues to be interpreted and handled within the context of internal rivalries, rather than in relation to the wider agenda outside. Often our churches are seen to be similarly consumed by internal rivalry and conflicts and not therefore properly engaged with issues in society. One of the reasons that clergy chapters sometimes struggle to function well, is the underlying currents of rivalry between those whose approaches to the task of leadership are very different. Beneath our Anglican politeness, there can be a dynamic of competition that is deeply destructive, with an implication that those who differ from me should 'keep silent'. The result is a concentration of attention and energy on the wrong things – the opposite of the demands of prophetic leadership. It is often easier to concentrate upon the domestic agendas of internal rivalry than to work together to engage with the missionary call of the word of the Lord.

As Elisha is drawn closer to Elijah through these defining encounters that highlight the temptations which can undermine prophetic leadership, so his own call is refined and tested further. In a definitive exhibition of leadership, Elijah parts the River Jordan and they walk across on dry land. Significantly, they leave a company of the prophets on the other side. Here is a real separation and calling to a particular ministry, distanced from the institutionalised approach to leadership. The latter served to emphasise the focus upon tradition and its transmission, but invariably developed ways of working that became systematised and less open to the breaking in of new life, with the different perceptions this produced. Prophetic leadership may benefit from some kind of academic formation, but its exercise is generally a lonely, wilderness based ministry.

Elisha is asked about the gifts he needs for this ministry and requests a double share of the spirit of Elijah. The prophet is always called to aim high, never to settle for a more ordinary, workable vision. The latter inevitably becomes the stuff of political leadership: it always needs to be in a challenging dialogue with the word of the Lord, that requires us to risk our apparent peace and stability for renewal and further grace, often involving the opening up of a greater inclusivity for the people of God. The agenda of the prophet is God's agenda – vital to be mixed in with the worldly agenda that presents itself for shaping and ordering. The Hebrew does not mean twice as much, but refers to 'the double portion of the eldest son' – a recognition of continuity and responsibility, rather than a personal gifting.

Elijah has crossed the Jordan to enter into his exodus. As they continue walking, he is separated from Elisha by fire and ascends into heaven. An image of crucifixion (fire which separates (consumes) and resurrection (ascension into heaven). The fire destroys and liberates his human life. This is a sign from the Lord to Elisha and the fundamental indication of how God can work in His world to cleanse and renew, often at cost to the way of living that has become normative and settled. To be a witness of this moment of crucifixion and resurrection, of consumption and ascension, of separation and at-one-ment, is to be made an apostle of the good news of the salvation God longs to offer. This is how His listening heart responds to the call of human struggle and limitation. Elisha experiences this defining moment and it provides the foundation and the consecration of his own prophetic leadership.

Elisha parts the Jordan and comes back to the company of the prophets. He is to withdraw and engage. This is the pattern in which he has been schooled. The company of highly trained prophets insist upon searching for the body of Elijah – they want to capture and control what has happened and keep it within the terms of their ability to interpret and understand. They want to maintain a very tight frame within which they are willing to receive any new life. Prophetic leadership easily becomes anti-prophetic, not merely political. They would like to honour Elijah's body and place it within their theology and tradition. As Elisha recognised, resurrection brings new life that cannot be trapped in such human tombs.

Only when they had failed to find the body could the company of the prophets be confronted with a more revolutionary truth – the miracle of resurrection. They knew about death, as burial. They had yet to learn about resurrection through fire – the gateway to ascension and glory. Prophetic leadership says 'do not go' in search of controlling all we experience: rather it invites a constant interchange between the two worlds we are able to inhabit – the seen and the unseen, the outer and the inner.

The chapter ends with two strange incidents, both of which serve to bring Elisha's prophetic leadership firmly down to earth. First the community with bad water. This is the lot of many people still on our planet. In these circumstances, there is limited interest in the agenda of the company of prophets – the theological debate and the conserving of tradition. Most of God's children simply seek a means of survival – basic things like water, work, welfare.

Elisha does not dig a new well, or make alternative arrangements. He simply enacts a sign, using salt. A resonance with the teaching of Jesus about the contribution the gospel can make, through signs, and through small but decisive interventions such as the adding of salt or leaven. Elisha does not change what the community already has, he simply adds something that effects a transformation. In modern terms, a strategic intervention. He begins with real needs and adds something that is sharp, abrasive and transformative. He does not stand safely on one side and offer a prayer or a blessing – he does something tangible which makes a difference. The prophetic leader is inspired to discern what kind of enacted contribution might be transformative for the wellbeing of the community.

Finally, the incident with the small boys shouting 'baldy'. To stand in a distinctive place is to invite not just attention, but sometimes insult and opposition. It comes with the territory of being a vicar. Sometimes we ignore or deflect these attacks. But sometimes they should be confronted. Elisha curses the boys in the name of the Lord. He prays for God to judge, he does not pronounce or act himself. He challenges them in the name of the Lord. As a result, two she-bears appear and maul or lacerate his attackers.

Should we ignore such a narrative, as Marcion advised? Rather, we need to take seriously the reality of God's judgment, especially in relation to human arrogance and aggression. The prophetic leader is not alone amidst such attacks, sometimes the pain is to be absorbed, but sometimes God acts to challenge and cleanse and change. Our task is to bring these pressures to the Lord and not pronounce or act ourselves.

Lastly Elisha goes to Mount Carmel. The key to prophetic leadership is the bedrock discipline of withdrawal into the wilderness, away from the tumultuous world he is called to serve, into a prayerful space of humility and dependence.

CHAPTER - 14

The Gospel of Prophetic Leadership

II Kings 4

Elisha had been ordained into prophetic leadership through his experience of death and resurrection – when Elijah was taken from this life and raised into heaven. This was the basis of the Gospel to which he was called to witness.

In this chapter, we can observe how he ministers this Gospel in a variety of encounters. The first story involves the unending flow of oil. Elisha encourages the widow to trust in the resources that she clearly has, rather than seek for new ones. Through this gift God can provide. The normal, measurable criteria of political organisation and calculation can be confounded by the sheer generosity and graciousness of God's new life flowing towards us. The prophetic leader is sometimes able to discern such power and encourage others to trust and receive it. The key transaction is between God and the widow, the prophet offers a new perspective and confidence that encourages her to connect the cry of her heart with the grace of her maker and redeemer.

The wealthy woman in Shunem provides another set of insights. Shunem had been a Philistine camp. Now it was to be a place of revelation. God's new life is not just to be met in set apart holy places, but in the most unlikely people and situations. This is a major sub text in the ministry of Jesus too.

The woman is wealthy. In one sense, she has everything that she needs, and yet she is conscious of a deep lack. This is the territory of spiritual discernment – exposing the deeper needs to be owned as a cry of the human heart. She knows that there is a deeper need and this is the source of her fascination with this holy person. She builds a relationship with him, offering food and the support of her household. She does not yet articulate her deepest need, but she engages Elisha in what we can recognise as a pastoral relationship.

Next she suggests to her husband that they provide a 'small roof chamber'. She recognises this holy person as a resource provided by God and she wants to invest in the resource. At this stage, her relationship is with the prophet, rather than directly with God. He acts as mediator and representative. Many of us experience this kind of vicarious spirituality. There may not be an obvious awareness of God, but there can be an increasing engagement with what God provides. So she invests in 'church and ministry' – that is in building a holy space and providing someone to inhabit it. The key is the roof chamber. She is not looking for parity or friendship, in modern terms she is looking for dependency. She puts the prophet on the roof, above her and her household – closer to heaven. She is conscious that there is some kind of distance between herself and God, between herself and the instruments that God provides.

Many people need the mediating ministry of something that is 'holy' (whole), whether a person, a place, a scripture. Spiritual engagement proceeds through negotiating the distance between the cry of the human heart and the fuller potential of God's blessing and wholeness. It is important not to undermine this vital and life-giving dynamic by focussing upon a pastoral mode of relationship, which too easily closes the gap and creates a sense of mutuality and friendship. Both the pastoral and the prophetic approaches have their place. But in order to draw out the deepest cries of the human heart, there often needs to be a mediator who stands apart – in the space between the struggling, seeking soul and the gracious goodness of God.

In many ways, the church building fulfils a similar role, because its whole atmosphere and resources are so different from the domestic spaces which we normally inhabit. There can be a danger in making church too user-friendly – it enhances the quality of pastoral relationship, but this can be a barrier to prophetic encounter. The spiritual journey needs to be especially located outside the city wall, on the way to somewhere else.

The woman desires a representative, someone who can be 'on behalf of' her and her household – a vicarious person: a vicar. Someone who can provide more focus and depth for the presence and power of God and negotiate the distance she feels from the fullness of such holiness or wholeness.

Elisha asks the key question: 'what can be done for you?' He begins with the obvious desires of the heart, recognition, affirmation, connection with power and privilege. She is content on all these fronts. It is Elisha's servant Gehazi who helps articulate the real cry of her heart 'she has no son'. The role of the pastoral assistant can be crucial!

This conversation takes place as she stands in the doorway, on the edge of the holy space. Elisha is inside, she lives outside, but comes to the edge, the boundary, the 'Porch'.

This is where most people stand in relation to the church and in relation to her ministers. They seek help to articulate their deepest desires, to own the distance they feel from wholeness and grace and to seek mediation and connection. This is the place of spiritual transaction.

Too often the worship we offer, the experience of stepping across the boundary into the Assembly, becomes disconnected from this profound, prophetic moment of spiritual encounter and rather settles into a comforting confirmation of a new status quo. The Assembly of public worship can become an alternative household in itself, rather than a deeper engagement with the mystery of distance, disconnection and yet the desire for connection and blessing.

One of the most popular activities for those who enter our churches, especially for 'outsiders' is to light candles. A small flame illuminates the 'edge' of life and new life, concentrates thoughts and feelings into prayer and seeks an atmosphere which is totally different from the domestic spaces we normally occupy. This kind of activity negotiates the boundary between earth and heaven as did the woman standing in the doorway of the prophet: sacred space.

Her deepest desire is for a son. For new life against the odds. This is what every human being desires. It is not simply a story about infertility, as modern interpretations might observe. This encounter is a sign of the engagement of prophetic leadership with the everyday life of the people of God. The deepest cry in any human heart is for new life against the odds. For a wholeness that always seems beyond our reach, no matter how well organised or 'successful' our outward (political) lives seem to be.

The task of prophetic leadership is to help her articulate this cry of the heart and to invite her to accept the miracle of the birth of new life against the odds. The same thing happened to the fishermen Jesus called to be apostles.

This desire is so deep that the woman initially denies it. The prophet needs wisdom both to challenge with the invitation and to persevere when the apparent evidence points in the opposite direction. It is important to have the courage not to take what people say at face value – especially with regard to God and the Gospel. Gehazi the pastoral assistant also has a role to play.

The woman becomes pregnant and bears a child; she is the agent of bringing new life into the world. The child grows and thrives. Suddenly he is taken ill and dies. The spiritual path, the gift of new life is never smooth and successful. Prophetic leadership should know this truth from experience. This is the exact story of another Son.

The woman has to learn that she does not own this new life, she is merely a guardian. We cannot sustain the life God gives us, we can only have it sustained by receiving God's grace, which is accessed through the resources He provides – ministry, sacraments, creeds and scriptures. The ingredients that make holy places and holy persons so distinctive. As a priest, one is only part of the resourcing which God provides.

When the son dies, the woman does not seek solace from her husband, or from Gehazi the pastoral assistant. She keeps praying the refrain 'all will be well'. She does not bury the son (as generally happened in that climate). She lays him in the holy place – the place where heaven and earth interact. And she sets off to find the prophet, the mediator and interpreter of wholeness, of God's greater agenda. In a similar way, we lay the body of the dead son on the altar in the Eucharist, and pray to the Father.

The son's fleshliness has been destroyed, in order to be re-born as God's gift. This is the mystery that Nicodemus failed to understand. The gift of life easily becomes colonised and corrupted by our attempts to preserve and control what we have received. It needs to be offered back to God, in all its fractured frailty, so that by the miraculous gift of His life giving spirit, it can be renewed and fully redeemed. This is the process we call Eucharist. It is the pattern of the spiritual journey that prophetic leadership is called to encounter and to invite others to experience. Life has to be offered back to God, taken, broken, to be blessed and renewed for the service of all His people – a distribution of His new life for others.

The woman goes to Mount Carmel. She follows the spiritual path into the wilderness, the place of concentrated prayer. She refuses the pastoral ministry of Gehazi. Her conversation, like that of Mary with Jesus outside the tomb, is not one between friends; it is formal, focussed on the mystery of death and life. Such an encounter goes beyond the personal, into the place of revelation. Prophetic leadership must sometimes resist the temptation to set the bar lower and collude in pastoral conversation. The stakes may be higher: the gospel of death and life.

The church gathered to minister this gospel, has, therefore, to be more than a fellowship. It is a place of dependency, crying out, seeking new life against the odds. A place of tough spiritual confrontation. Too much of my own ministry tends to avoid this prophetic challenge for the softer key of pastoral togetherness.

Elisha here learns the foundational lesson imported to Elijah in similar circumstances. He goes to the holy place; he prays to the Lord and breathes his life into him. There is an element of proper ritual. The child sneezes seven times as a sign of the completion of receiving new breath and new life. The household has learned that God's fuller life depends upon offering ourselves to be born again in the power of His Holy Spirit. The ritual is important because it confirms that this renewal into true life is not the result of Elisha's ministry, rather it was the gift of God. Elisha had acted as mediator and interpreter.

The chapter ends with Elisha transforming the nourishment of a community whose collective arrangements were otherwise going to poison human life. He uses a handful of flour rather than salt!

But, once again, from a dramatic moment of ministering the Gospel of Resurrection from the dead, he is called to engage with mundane, everyday issues of survival and effective organisation of community life. Prophetic leadership operates across the full spectrum between these two kinds of need.

Finally, he helps a community confront the limitations of the human ability to make provision for growth and welfare, but inviting them, once again, to use what resource they already possess, in a way that trusts the word of the Lord. All will be well and they are enabled to find a way of sharing their resources that provides for their own needs and also creates a surplus. Grace is often signified by the problem of overabundance. Prophetic leadership invites serious engagement with this mystery. Political leadership is left with the challenge of how to handle a surplus. Not by building bigger barns.

CHAPTER - 15

Keeping the Distance

II Kings 5

aaman is the king of Aram's military commander. He represents the kingly model of leadership exercised through political and military power, and an official religion to encourage coherence and a common sense of direction. He has been very successful within this framework, ensuring security and stability – the pragmatism of peace. But, he suffers from leprosy. Despite his success in ordering the stability and security of human fleshly living, he has a constant reminder of the frailty of the flesh, the reality of our vulnerability and imperfection. In a literal sense, flesh does decay, despite the contrary signals so energetically given out by political systems. Each of us should learn to live with this truth. Flesh is frail and decays. This is why empires rise and fall, as do individual lives, even churches.

Then there is a young Israelite slave; in exile, at a distance from her people, and from those amongst who she lives. This distance enables her to offer a new perspective. Alongside the reality of political success and the reality of fleshly frailty, there is another factor that can be brought into this seemingly irreconcilable paradox – the prophetic leadership that God raises up amongst His people. Her place in the story is prophetic in itself. Wisdom was normally associated with the elderly and with men. Here God calls a young girl, a slave, to begin the process of prophetic leadership. From all these unlikely sources there emerges someone whose own spiritual journey is rooted in being set apart, in the 'wilderness' of a foreign place, dependent and distant.

Quite properly within the neat systems of political organisation, Naaman takes this advice to the King, the person in charge. He decides to deal with the King of Israel. This is how political systems work. Each system will order its resources for its own benefit. Power speaks to power.

The King of Israel knows the limitations of political power. He may be able to order human lives to produce peace and prosperity, but he cannot cure leprosy. His success may help people ignore the reality of the decay of the flesh, but he knows that this is an illusion – one that people like political leadership to provide.

However, he does not think to consult the prophet. He simply interprets this request within the limited political framework of the contest for power and control. He despairs at what he sees to be an act of aggression, challenging him to meet an impossible demand. Institutional frameworks are his only resource.

But Elisha can provide a different perspective; as usual he is at a distance from the court, from the central operation of political and religious power. But he offers the resources of prophetic leadership. Naaman is to go not to the centre of political power, but to the prophet – into the space which is on the edge, at a distance. He invites Naaman to 'go and wash in the Jordan seven times'. He is to go into a special place and be cleansed. The symbolism is important. Water, a crucial sign of new life in such a dry land. Jordan, a flowing stream of living water. Seven times indicates completion and wholeness. There is an essential ritual and rhythm that opens us to spiritual encounter and ensures that the power we meet is nothing to do with the one who acts as minister, but is always the direct gift of the grace of God. Ministers invite access to grace through sacraments. Prophetic leadership does not open up huge one-off events, it enables engagement with the normal working of a Gospel that longs to transform the decay of the flesh into the new life of eternity. Moreover the encounter is to occur in a public setting, not in some private or specialist clinic.

Naaman's initial response is processed through the lense of his political and military world. He is not interested in signs and symbolism, nor in undertaking such simple instructions from a prophet who is so distant that he does not even meet him. He expects a more rational and measurable approach: meeting, examination of the evidence, diagnosis, prescribed way of dealing with the issues identified. Politics works by human assessment and appropriate action.

However, at a more profound level, human hearts cry out with deeper needs than those that can be met by effective organisation and the handling of particular problems. We seek a different kind of connection and wholeness, with each other and with the ultimate purposes and possibilities in life. Often these needs can be highlighted and met through sacramental moments - gatherings for Jubilee celebrations or community events. Liturgy is designed to call out and minister to such needs with resources of word and sacrament – interpretation and sign.

What challenged Naaman and changed his mind? His servants, those used to dealing with ordinary things, like water, and also used to living by faith and dependency on others. They were distanced from the stability and security enjoyed by those 'in power'. Beneath the institutionalised framework of political organisation are many who are closer to knowing the realities of the spiritual journey and the importance of the challenge presented by the prophetic element.

Naaman submits to word and sacrament and his flesh is perfectly restored. A sign of the gift of new life against all the odds. He had to vacate the highly ordered, sophisticated world of political leadership and submit to what was 'river water religion' – something that was simple, free, flowing, not owned or controlled by church or state. God provided these resources and God was able to use them as agents of new life. Prophetic and political leadership could simply turn to them with the cry of the human heart and be renewed. Almost as basic as our salvation being located in bread and wine.

The prophet points to the place and the process of encounter and salvation (salvus: health). He points away from himself, to the signs that God has chosen to offer. There is no 'control' or efficient system, simply an invitation to 'taste and see that the Lord is good' (Ps 34). He has not negotiated his authority through pastoral relationships, he has simply taken the authority of his office and pointed the person in need to the resources God provides. Too often we locate our leadership in our pastoral skills and the resulting 'political' organisation of people and situations. In fact, leadership needs to be more confidently located in our role or office, and the priority of word and sacrament that God offers.

The key encounter takes place at the door of Elisha's household. On the boundary is the place of encounter and operation. This boundary is made and maintained by Elisha's discipline in keeping a distance from the centres of political organisation. Something to challenge how we handle the dynamic between the church gathered for worship or meetings and the importance of 'retreat' into more of a wilderness setting to be renewed in prioritising a greater and less 'domestic' perspective.

Naaman wishes to express his thanks. To give something back. The prophet refuses to receive anything for himself – this would confuse God's gift and grace with his own role. But he allows Naaman to take some soil, so that his new spiritual experience can continue to be 'earthed' in the moment of blessing, healing and revelation.

Nonetheless, he cannot escape into some pure, holy world. He must return to the limited and sometimes corrupt context of his own people's political and religious arrangement. New life from God does not create a separated cocoon of purity. Rather it equips us to engage in the fallenness of the world as witnesses to richer possibilities. This is part of the good news that prophetic leadership brings to church and to society. Rimmon will always exist. We need to offer support and play our part, always compromised, but eager to offer ourselves as leaven, salt, silent witnesses to a better way.

I suspect that many people shy away from our invitation because they know the impossibility of being totally 'pure'. Prophetic leadership should challenge this fantasy, and encourage recognition of the fact that we all continue to be sinners and therefore the spiritual journey of the Christian, like that of the prophet, will always be through trial, unevenness and challenge. The need for the cleansing and renewal of the flesh continues. Word and sacrament do not provide a one-off cure: they remain resources for a continuing journey. This is good news not just for us, but for the world of Rimmon too.

Elisha ends the encounter with the words 'Go in Peace'. The peace of God, not the artificial and pragmatic peace of political arrangements. He sends Naaman back to his own community, there is no invitation to join a special, select community of those blessed more directly with the gift of new life. The gift is to create salt and leaven – not a false separated security – which is too often the pathway of religious communities. Prophetic leadership enables freedom for the journey; it never calls into a particular conformity.

The final narrative shows that Gehazi, the pastoral assistant, is horrified that his idealistic 'vicar' has refused any contribution to the work of the Gospel. He knows that this work is costly, that Naaman longs to give something back and therefore pursues him and receives money and goods. His short-sightedness puts the material and organisational needs of 'the church'; first – this must be the platform for further witness. He has failed to see that Naaman was challenged 'to give something back' in terms of his own witness and disciplined spiritual journey. To confuse this offering of himself into the work of the Lord with supporting the church and its ministers was a terrible mistake. The theology of this approach is to feel that God does not actually just give the grace, rather He trades. He expects a certain return on His investment. Again, this is a very widespread misconception. A theology that grace is earned, and then must be preserved in special set apart communities to maintain purity.

As a sign of having to recognise the necessary frailty of the church as an organisation, Gehazi is struck down with leprosy himself. He will need to pursue the path he has been privileged to observe the prophet and so many of those to whom he ministers to follow. A shift from dependency upon making our own arrangements and organisation, to crying out from the depths of the heart in humility and utter dependence. Every exercise of prophetic leadership should end with this blessing in a new freedom: 'Go in peace'.

CHAPTER - 16

Prophecy Shaping Politics
II Kings 6

Elisha is visiting 'the company of the prophets', the place of formation to provide prophetic leadership for the people of God. Like his master, and mentor Elijah, he was perhaps used as some kind of visiting lecturer, or even an overseer – they owned to being under his charge. As within many institutions, they were outgrowing their current arrangements, and seeking to mark this growth by taking steps to become more permanently established. Always a dangerous strategy for prophecy! They wanted to build log cabins, more permanent structures which could be designed for the provision of better facilities.

They decide to undertake the building work themselves. They do not organise a series of fundraising events, they choose to make their own provision. A sign of poverty and possibly of determined self-sufficiency. One of the students has borrowed an axe head, which falls into the water. Iron was a valuable commodity. To replace the axe head could have been very expensive, especially for a poor and self-sufficient group of scholars. One way of interpreting this incident is to recognise that the borrowing of the axe head points to a degree of partnership with the local community and a need to honour the mutual obligations thereby created. If we operate through partnership, we need to be trustworthy and honourable, so that what we achieve can be appreciated and recognised by others.

Another approach to the narrative is to recognise an act of resurrection through water. Think of Naaman dipping his decaying body in the water. Its inevitable trajectory was downwards, sinking towards death and oblivion. The same might be said of Jonah as he was first thrown into the sea and then swallowed by the fish. This is the sign of Baptism – dipped down into the water towards death, only to be raised up, cleansed and renewed. The death and resurrection of Jesus similarly confounded the 'laws' of nature – beyond any evidence or measurable human experience.

So, in this story, the prophet points to an act of resurrection through water, against all the odds. This is an important part of the whole building project. God does not simply build with wood or brick and mortar. He builds through us and our partnerships and He builds through a spiritual presence which can be transformative and offering power that raises new life and possibilities even beyond the norms of our usual experience and expectations. The result is a sense of power and purpose and of blessing that can raise our sights above what might seem to be easily manageable from our own resources.

Here is a lesson about how to construct public space for theology, for schooling in prophetic leadership. We offer our own commitment and endeavours, we solicit support and partnership with others and we are open to the transformative power and presence of God. A project that illustrates the path of the spiritual journey that prophetic leadership summons us to follow: opening our hearts to identify our real needs, receiving help and encouragement (new life) from others and being blessed together in ways that witness to the sheer saving grace and goodness of God.

Having explored once again the foundations that continually form and re-form prophetic leadership, Elisha is called to make his witness in the public square, in relation to the King of Aram. The prophet is able to offer a fuller perspective upon the movements of the time, including an identification of the strategic manoeuvres of the King of Aram as he sought to position himself to ensure success in his struggle against the King of Israel. Two political systems in conflict, disputing about structures of power and control. One of these is blessed by the presence of a prophet and is able to avoid being drawn into a simple confrontation of military might.

When the King of Aram discovers that it is the prophetic leadership of Elisha that is thwarting his plans to pursue his aims through the deployment of naked power, he pursues the prophet to the town of Dothan.

The advice and guidance of Elisha is maintaining a different kind of peace and stability. Not one dependent upon military force, but one that emerges for operating within the wider perspective of God's agenda for peace for all His people. An agenda that calls for the avoidance of crude confrontation. This prophetic approach does not solve the problem; it simply invites the King of Israel to begin the path of a different journey. One that is not clearly marked out in advance, but one that will follow the way of a prophet's spiritual walk and emerge in an unexpected gift of new life.

The King of Aram resents this intrusion of the interpretative power of religion and the guidance that it gives to the heart. He wants to conquer and thus extend his existing kingdom. He sends his army to surround the town of Dothan, to capture Elisha and silence the voice of the prophet. Politics seeks to capture and subdue religion. This has always been the ideal relationship from the point of view of the politician. Religion must be used to reinforce political arrangements, not thwart them. Otherwise peace will become impossible. Today many people see religion as a force which brings chaos and confusion. There is a huge temptation for religion to settle for an honourable role in the political system – generally at the cost of abandoning the priority of a prophetic call rooted in the mystery of death and resurrection.

Elisha refuses to compromise. His companion is terrified by this ferocious display of political power that is determined to get its own way – with no argument and no compromise. He can only evaluate it in the political terms of the times, force can only be countered by force and on this occasion, the weakness of the prophet will mean submission and defeat.

Elisha has to teach him that though surrounded by such a display of political power, when the servant asks 'what shall we do?', the answer is 'nothing'. The prophet has to take no defensive or offensive action. His approach transcends that of the political and the military. Just as Jesus refuses to allow His companions to fight in the Garden of Gethsemane. He could have appealed to the Father to send legions of angels – the power of goodness and guidance that God deploys.

Rather the prophet prays 'O Lord, please open his eyes that he may see'. The servant was able to observe the mountain full of horses and chariots of fire – the forces of death and resurrection that Elisha had experienced with Elijah. The power of God is very different. It is not political power that crushes and dominates. It is unseen, but much more effective. As the servant of Elisha had his eyes open to see this power, so the Arameans were confirmed in their blindness, their inability to see anything clearly beyond their own needs and appetites. This is a selfish, sterile way of living.

Elisha the prophet takes advantage of such monumental short-sightedness, and he is able to lead this vast army into Samaria, the heart of their enemies' territory. They are led away from the area of conflict and conquest.

The reaction of the King of Israel is to further his own selfish aims and kill the enemies thus delivered to him. Elisha is clear that in their blindness, the Arameans have been captured by God, not by the King of Israel. The prophetic leader challenges the political leader to abandon his own selfish short-sightedness and to become an agent of God's renewing grace and generosity. Rather than killing his enemies, he is to provide them with a feast of fellowship. Food and drink are to be set before them. Just as the ministry of Jesus unfolded, not through confrontation, but through table fellowship, which even included Judas and Peter, both of whom were to betray Him.

Enemies are made friends in a Eucharistic feast – joined by God's grace and God's provision. A Eucharistic moment, which undermines the political aspirations of conquest and domination and creates a dynamic of mutuality that ensures not only the safe return of the Arameans to their homeland, but also the strengthening of a spirit which produced peace. "They no longer come raiding into the land of Israel".

The blindness that made others enemies was softened and enlightened. Arameans and Israelites were able to inhabit political systems which were less insecure, less aggressive, more content to walk in the way of a new life of peacefulness.

But in a fallen world, peace is precarious. Political ambition becomes more strident and competitive. The King of Aram invades Samaria. There is a siege, famine and desperation. Children being eaten. A terrible contrast to the guidance of prophetic leadership which enabled these enemies to share table fellowship together. Now the prophet is blamed for the new chaos. Religion is expected to deliver goodness, a perfect society. Any re-emergence of unevenness and violence is seen not as a failing of political organisation and leadership, but as a failing of religion which promises so much and seems to deliver so little. This unevenness of fallen human beings provides the greatest challenge to prophetic leadership.

The story of Solomon illustrated both the potential for religion to shape politics with wisdom and a frame within which people could be fulfilled. The delivery of growth and welfare. Yet even Solomon fell from this place of perfection. There is a serious problem of sustainability for political systems. If religion is too closely allied with a particular approach, its own contribution will be equally limited and disappointing.

Even prophetic leadership has proved to be unsustainable and subject to the temptations and unevenness of any human endeavour. Elisha is simply able to counsel patience and trust. He knows that God is ultimately faithful, but not within the timings that might seem to suit humankind, and not without the re-forming journey of renewal that we are called to follow as challenges beset us. There is to be no direct action, no further trust in political processes, or military might. Patience through huge suffering, a kind of Holy Week journey, will see God deliver salvation, though not without cost to Himself and to His children.

In Elisha, we can identify some of the key marks of prophetic leadership.

First it has the courage to interpret the political world in which we are set.

Next, it has the courage to point to signs of success and blessing and also to endure suffering and judgment by the world. This is the area of the fire which refines, separates, consumes and raises up to new life as sheer and unexpected gift.

The key is to trust in God's grace and goodness and in God's different way of doing things, even through suffering and death. God can create peace even between enemies, through common participation in the Eucharistic feast, the table fellowship through which our needs and differences are met. At times we will degenerate into chaos, so that people's children are consumed, but we have to hold on in trust and faithfulness, even against the apparent evidence.

The prophetic leader needs to know when to speak or act and when to wait or retreat, or endure.

The invitation is always into a journey of heart crying out to heart, of fellowship in peacefulness and the chance to take these models of compromise and co-operation into the working world of political and religious life.

The temptation is always retreat into the relative clarity and security of political leadership, an area where it seems that there can be a continuity of control and effective management. Prophetic leadership, by contrast, is infinitely complex, incomplete, uneven and un-enduring. Yet is it the leadership through which the peace of God is best ministered.

Epilogue

The position of a priest involves leadership that is both political and prophetic. The organisation of parish and Parochial Church Council: the proclamation of the Gospel of God's grace.

This series of studies has explored the possibilities and the pitfalls of these different demands in leadership, and has also begun to examine the potential tensions and complementarities between them.

Throughout the discussions, there was widespread recognition of the value of successful systems and spaces for organisation and negotiation, together with the ownership of a strong temptation to make this approach to leadership 'normative' and ensuring its maintenance through pastoral engagement. Such an emphasis very easily shifts into determining the pattern and style of liturgy – well organ and pastorally sensitive. Growth and welfare are important goals that can be effectively pursued by these means. 'Political' leadership can establish clear markers for performance, participation and priorities. People value the clarity and direction that can result. Mission Action Planning can provide a suitable tool to ensure thoughtful and appropriate delivery. The 'Gospel' is used to provide inspiration and examples of the negotiation of peace and harmony, justice and fairness, collegiality and identify.

Many of these marks of the 'political' element in leadership can have the effect of strengthening a sense of valuable fellowship, focussed on clear identity and boundaries (around belief, behaviour or both). It can also provide a clear and attractive witness to those outside of the gathered fellowship, who naturally inhabit a similarly 'political' world where values and markers are expressed in terms of the effectiveness of organisation and communication that can provide the sacred trinity so important to a this-worldly agenda – growth, welfare and peace.

The more 'prophetic' elements of the Gospel and of the commissioned task of the ordained minister, tend to be deployed around particular causes and moments of crisis. They are rarely part of the regular way in which leadership and discipleship unfold. Prophetic leadership can easily be marginalised into the largest macro picture about values, such as ecological issues or the desire for peace and justice amidst horrendous conflict - or into very specific micro areas of personal or small group behaviour.

The study of the books of Kings reveals a much more mundane dynamic between the political and the prophetic aspects of leadership. The tendency to gather, to focus, to offer identity, security and stability (the fruits of political leadership) can lead to exclusion, false boundaries and a narrowing down of God's kingdom agenda. It can also lead towards a spirituality which becomes safely repetitive and unadventurous.

By contrast, the prophetic leadership in Kings is crucial to maintaining a concentration upon the nature of the spiritual journey we are invited to make. It is honest about unevenness, the centrality of the deepest cry of the human heart and the articulation and acting out of a genuine humility, dependency and sense of incompletion before the mystery of a love that offers renewal – not as a secure and totally achieved state of being, but as an ever unfolding sense of significant encounters. Each encounter can contribute to individuals, groups and nations being led into a confidence to cross the normal defensive boundaries and engage more fully with 'others' – including engagement with the most unexpected and unusual people and causes.

This is a different kind of 'peace' – not organised by human skills, but received as a surprising gift of new life. The gift is to be treasured - but the 'peace' is not immune to the further irruptions that the frailty and unevenness of human being produce. Prophetic leadership invites engagement with insights and signs – word and sacrament – to enable a cleansing, renewing, re-shaping which gives direction and encouragement for the continuing journey. The prophetic leader acts as mediator, from a distance, expressing a spiritual journey that they themselves are walking: the outcome of such leadership is the more direct engagement of others with the grace and mercy of God.

The clearer identification of these two elements of leadership emerges from the narrative in I and II Kings because, apart from the story of Solomon, the roles of 'politician' and 'prophet' tend to be found in different people. This separation allows us to examine each approach in some detail, including their essential inter-relation and inter-dependence.

However, for a priest in the contemporary church, the complexity is our commission to fulfil both roles – in one office. The model for ordination is that of the Good Shepherd. Part of this brief is political: to organise proper nourishment and security for the sheep to flourish. Growth, welfare and peace are essential aims and outcomes for this part of the Shepherd's commission. Yet the Good Shepherd is also called to a more 'prophetic' role – to discover new contexts that can be places of creative engagement for the flock, and also, most distinctively for a Christian gospel, to bring in new sheep – those at present outside and excluded.

These two tasks need to inform each other. There is an inevitable temptation to concentrate upon the task at hand - the wellbeing of the existing flock. Often this can seem to be daunting enough on its own. We only need to face major repairs to the sheep fold! And in an age of hyper self-sensitivity, the pastoral demand of each member for expert care and guidance can be all-consuming – even if one raises up other helpers into a leadership team.

But the primary purpose is God's love for the world. His desire to embrace all His children more directly. This prophetic commission involves not simply engagement on the edge, or beyond the established territories of the existing flock, it also requires the wisdom and insight to identify the changes, the renewal and re-formation that might better enable those called into discipleship to make this mission the prime priority. It is clear from I and II Kings that the prophetic leader is not expected to provide 'answers' or worked out, improved alternatives to the current 'political' arrangements. The task is more subtle and should give space for God to encounter and act with others. Hence the role involves a modelling of the spiritual journey and an offering of this possibility into situations of stress or of opportunity.

The tools are those of word and sacrament. Interpretation of the present through a disciplined immersion in the tradition, the established ways in which God offers His faithfulness. Complemented by an openness to the signs, the moments and issues through which this invitation to articulate the deepest cry of the heart, in humility and dependency, can be offered. Those who step out on such a spiritual journey will be encountered by the miracle of God's grace, the blessing of new life – not as an 'answer', but as a sign of His ultimate power and purpose.

The Good Shepherd models each of these approaches to leadership. It can be done! And sometimes we are able to combine these elements of our role in ways which maintain the security, stability and peace of those gathered into the assembly, while offering challenge and a route to transforming encounter (change) that will re-shape existing arrangements in order to enable wider participation. This is a process that needs to be continually pursued. Every successful shift soon becomes a normalised system to be defended as the key to continuing growth and welfare. In fact, any continuation of growth and welfare on these terms will only serve to provide artificial protection for the community and barriers for those outside. Each renewal of 'political' organisation needs a period of consolidation and then a moment of prophetic challenge to re-shape and respond to new possibilities of the continuing and ever widening offer of God's love and grace.

It may be possible to identify this vital dynamic between the two poles of leadership that we have examined through this study at I and II Kings. However, it remains a task of enormous challenge to try to inhabit both roles as a way of knowing our call and commission to serve the Good Shepherd in having responsibility for the ordering and mission of the church. Clearly none of us can ever begin to fulfil this double commission in our own strength, but in some political leaders and in some prophetic leaders in our chosen narrative, we can recognise the amazing way in which God consecrates and equips people to fulfil these tasks. We must trust in His guidance and be disciplined in giving priority to working with the Lord, so that in His power, we can fulfil His forming and re-forming of His church and of His people. That is our privilege, to be trusted to share in the divinely designed leadership of the people of God.